Sundays with Sophie

Sundays with Sophie

*Flay Family Recipes for
Any Day of the Week*

Bobby Flay

with Emily Timberlake
and Inspiration from Sophie Flay

Photographs by Ed Anderson

Clarkson Potter/Publishers
New York

This book is dedicated to Sophie's mom, my parenting partner, Kate Connelly.

Contents

— " —

My dad is an amazing teacher. He's dedicated his life to teaching his employees, his friends, his family, and his fans how to cook.

I've picked up a few things here and there along the way, just by being near him. As a little girl, my signature spot was the table in a booth next to the kitchen at Mesa Grill in New York City. I would sit there for hours: waiting, watching, eating, and learning. Waiting for my dad to send out multiple scoops of ice cream or the latest creation from his talented pastry chef. Watching jaw-dropping guests come through for lunch, like former First Lady Michelle Obama with her beautiful daughters and mother. Eating a slightly edited version of a dish called the "Sophie Chopped Salad" (see Anatomy of a Chopped Salad, page 182) because my palate wasn't quite ready for the taste of lettuce yet. But the one thing I've learned from him in the kitchen and at the dining table is to be curious. Don't be afraid to ask questions about food and culture. Don't be afraid to try something you've never eaten before. Jump at those opportunities with curiosity and with an open mind. When it comes to food, no question is a bad one. It allows us to learn and grow as taste testers and cooks. Food is the pathway to better understanding one another. And with that in mind, I'm always excited to be a student in his kitchen.

— " —

Introduction

Sitting down to eat a meal on any Sunday is really satisfying to me, even before we start to eat. Whether it's breakfast, brunch, or dinner, I have a pretty relaxed attitude because Sunday is usually a day of rest, at least on some level. I probably don't have any appointments, Zoom meetings, or business calls scheduled. The only thing on my calendar is a date with my stove to cook some comforting dishes that will wind up at the center of my table. Even more important than the food are the people who will join me.

Cooking is my calling card. It's the way I show my love and appreciation for the important people in my life. My daughter, Sophie, is without a doubt at the head of my table. She's my only child, and I like to joke that her presence is mandatory, whether she likes it or not!

The title of this book might seem a little narrow at first blush. Don't take it literally. It's not just for one day of the week and it's not just things I cook for Sophie. Sophie's name graces the cover of this book because she is the person who is most important to me. But it is also a placeholder for all the people who are most important to you. And in this case, "Sunday" represents any day that calls for a table filled with delicious, easy-to-create dishes. It could be a holiday or party, the end of a tough week, or maybe it actually is Sunday dinner.

My family, friends, and close colleagues know that when I want to chat about something, I fire up my oven or my grill. If my goal is to capture people's attention, I know if I have them gathered around a table filled with their favorite dishes, I have a good shot at accomplishing that.

It's no secret that our complicated world has given us plenty to think about. Some people choose to have those conversations through social media or on other digital platforms. That's not for me. My important conversations take place around the table, face-to-face with a plate full of food and glass or two of my favorite wine. There's something old-school about it, and that's what I love. My dining table is a safe forum where we can debate, agree, disagree, laugh, cry, and celebrate. It's where my closest feel comfortable sharing their opinions and, personally, I've been enlightened when I didn't think it was possible. I give the food all the credit for keeping everyone in their seats!

I was inspired to write this book when I reflected on the thousands of meals and conversations I've shared with Sophie over the years, in so many settings and locations around the world. The book is a product of real-life moments with just the two us, whether we're sharing some good or troubling news, spilling family business, discussing our personal lives, or kicking around our career trials and tribulations. I cherish my close and honest relationship with my daughter. For the last twenty-five years or so, she's been the inspiration I've leaned on to keep me working as hard as I can to ensure she has the tools she needs to have a good life.

Of course, as a proud father I'm beyond impressed with Sophie's accomplishments, which are many, including her successful career as a community journalist in Los Angeles. But my favorite moments involve cooking and eating with her, because one thing we have in common is we're always hungry! We have very similar palates and favorites. Neither of us has seen a fish with a shell we didn't like, especially lobster, crab, shrimp, clams, and oysters. Hams, whether baked with a sweet and spicy glaze or cured in the style of Italy's prosciutto or Spain's serrano, have always been in our top ten. We even have similar taste in cocktails. Margaritas, martinis, and spritzes are our faves (although Sophie's Moscow Mule obsession is her own!).

In the pages that follow you'll find many of Sophie's and my home-cooked favorites from more than two decades of eating together, plus a handful of recipes that were created during the national quarantine of 2020. As always, I approach everything I cook with an eye toward flavor. I want your taste buds to sing with every bite, and for you to notice layers of textures that produce crispy, crunchy moments in every platter of food.

Along the way I thought about dishes and techniques that would help Sophie become a little more comfortable in the kitchen—she's got great taste and is very knowledgeable about food (she grew up in restaurants, after all), but she'll be the first to admit that she's not the most confident cook. So throughout the book I've sprinkled a few kitchen conversations and cooking lessons designed to help Sophie—or anyone else who is just finding their footing in the kitchen—master key basics. If you're about to send your kid away to college, give them this book so they can at least scramble an egg once they get there.

One of Sophie's nicest qualities is her spirit of inclusion. I can only hope it's one of the sensibilities she picked up from her father. While we love sharing meals just the two of us, we're even happier when we're joined by people we are close to or people we can't wait to meet. I hope the recipes in this book produce many wonderful moments between you and the people close to you, too. Just remember, if it's Sunday, there's a seat waiting at our table. Sophie and I will be expecting you.

Bobby Flay
In a kitchen somewhere

Breakfast and Brunch

Buttermilk Biscuits
with Fresh Blueberry Jam

I always have a carton of buttermilk in my refrigerator so I can make waffles, pancakes, or these biscuits. I never know when Sophie is going to roll into the house with a dozen of her crew for brunch; it's usually a last-minute event. But I'm armed with my buttermilk and always ready.

1. Set one oven rack in the upper third of the oven and a second oven rack in the bottom third of the oven and preheat the oven to 450°F. Line two baking sheets with parchment paper.

2. In a large bowl, combine the flour, baking powder, baking soda, and salt. Mix well, then incorporate the cold butter using your fingers or a pastry cutter until the mixture resembles coarse meal. Add the buttermilk and use your hands to gently mix until the mixture just begins to come together.

3. Scrape the dough onto a lightly floured counter. Pat the dough into a square ¾ inch thick. Cut the dough into equal squares (or rounds using a 3-inch round cutter). Press together the scraps and repeat the process to make 9 or 10 biscuits total.

4. Place the biscuits 2 inches apart on the prepared baking sheets, 4 or 5 biscuits per baking sheet. Brush the tops with the heavy cream and sprinkle with the pepper.

5. Bake the biscuits until lightly golden brown, 12 to 15 minutes, switching racks and rotating the baking sheets front to back halfway through the baking time. Transfer to a wire rack and let cool a few minutes before serving warm with the blueberry jam.

Makes 9 or 10 biscuits

4 cups all-purpose flour, plus more for shaping

4 teaspoons baking powder

1 teaspoon baking soda

1 teaspoon kosher salt

1½ sticks (6 ounces) cold unsalted butter, cut into small pieces

1½ cups very cold buttermilk, well shaken

¼ cup heavy cream

1 teaspoon freshly ground black pepper

Fresh Blueberry Jam (recipe follows), for serving

Fresh Blueberry Jam

Makes about 1 cup

2 cups blueberries
⅓ cup sugar
1 tablespoon fresh lemon juice
Finely grated zest of 1 lemon
½ teaspoon pure vanilla extract

1. In a small saucepan, combine the blueberries, sugar, and lemon juice. Bring to a simmer over medium heat and cook, stirring occasionally, until most of the berries have burst and the juices are slightly thickened, about 15 minutes.

2. Transfer to a bowl, then stir in the lemon zest and vanilla extract. Transfer to the refrigerator. You can serve the jam after chilling it for 30 minutes—it will be a bit runnier, like a compote—or let it set and thicken in the refrigerator overnight. For longer storage, transfer to an airtight container and store in the refrigerator for up to 2 weeks.

— 66 —

Literally no one makes better biscuits than my dad. These are a summer staple and remind me of watching the Kentucky Derby with him at home. Whenever he invites everyone over for a big Triple Crown race, he's making these biscuits. —SF

Cornbread

with Sweet Chili Butter

I make cornbread all summer long. It's always on my table whenever I serve barbecue anything. I like to slather the hot cornbread with some sort of sweetened butter, so when I found a bottle of a Thai sweet chili sauce in my refrigerator (left behind by my favorite recipe tester, Susie Vu), I knew I had to try it folded into butter. Just like that, I had a delicious new condiment for BBQ Day at my house. You can find Thai sweet chili sauce in jars in the Asian or international aisle of most grocery stores. Alternatively, you can mix 2 tablespoons of warmed honey with a pinch of red pepper flakes and add that to your butter.

1. In a small saucepan, melt 1 stick (4 ounces) of the butter over medium heat, 2 to 3 minutes. Remove from the heat and set aside.

2. In a small bowl, combine the remaining 1 stick (4 ounces) butter, sweet chili sauce, and ¼ teaspoon of the salt. Stir until smooth and set aside.

3. Set an oven rack in the middle position and preheat the oven to 450°F. Put a 10-inch cast-iron skillet in the oven for at least 10 minutes while you prepare the batter.

4. In a large bowl, stir together the cornmeal, flour, sugar, baking powder, baking soda, black pepper, and remaining 2 teaspoons salt.

5. In a small bowl, whisk together the eggs, buttermilk, and 6 tablespoons of the melted butter. Pour the buttermilk mixture into the cornmeal mixture and stir until just combined. Do not overmix.

6. Remove the skillet from the oven and carefully add the remaining 2 tablespoons melted butter, swirling the pan to coat. Scrape the batter into the hot pan and bake until lightly golden brown and a toothpick inserted into the center comes out clean, 16 to 20 minutes.

7. Let cool in the pan for 10 minutes, then remove from the pan, cut into wedges, and serve with the sweet chili butter.

Serves 8 to 10

2 sticks (8 ounces) unsalted butter, at room temperature

2 tablespoons Thai-style sweet chili sauce

2¼ teaspoons kosher salt

1½ cups stone-ground yellow cornmeal

½ cup plus 1 tablespoon all-purpose flour

2 tablespoons sugar

½ teaspoon baking powder

½ teaspoon baking soda

¼ teaspoon freshly ground black pepper

2 large eggs

1½ cups buttermilk, well shaken

Banana Bread
with Almond-Butter Butter

I rode the banana bread wave during the quarantine of 2020, as most people did. Bananas on their way out need a purpose and this is a delicious one. As a kid, peanut butter was an essential part of my after-school diet. Since then I've come to love other nut butters as well: almond, cashew, and my absolute fave, pistachio. Pick one, blend it with whole butter, and slather the resulting double butter on a slice of toasted banana bread while it's still warm.

1. Make the banana bread: Set an oven rack in the middle position and preheat the oven to 350°F. Liberally mist the bottom and sides of a loaf pan with cooking spray. Set aside.

2. In a large bowl, combine the all-purpose flour, almond flour, cane sugar, muscovado sugar, baking powder, cinnamon, baking soda, and fine salt. Whisk until well combined.

3. In a medium bowl, combine the melted butter, neutral oil, vanilla, bananas, and eggs. Whisk until smooth. Lightly fold the banana mixture into the flour mixture until just combined. The batter will be thick. Do not overmix or else the bread will be tough.

4. Scrape the batter into the prepared pan. Bake until the bread is golden brown and a toothpick inserted into the center comes out with a few moist crumbs attached, 50 minutes to 1 hour. Let the bread cool in the pan on a wire rack for 15 minutes, then remove the bread from the pan to cool completely.

5. Make the almond-butter butter: In a medium bowl, combine the butter, almond butter, honey, cinnamon, and kosher salt. Stir until smooth.

6. Serve the banana bread as is or toasted and slathered with the almond-butter butter.

Makes one 9-inch loaf

Banana Bread

Cooking spray, for the pan

1½ cups all-purpose flour

½ cup almond flour

½ cup pure cane sugar

¼ cup packed muscovado sugar or light brown sugar

1 teaspoon baking powder

½ teaspoon ground cinnamon

¼ teaspoon baking soda

¼ teaspoon fine salt

6 tablespoons unsalted butter, melted and cooled slightly

¼ cup neutral oil, such as avocado or canola

1 teaspoon pure vanilla extract

4 large overly ripe bananas, mashed well (about 1½ cups)

2 large eggs, lightly beaten

Almond-Butter Butter

6 tablespoons unsalted butter, at room temperature

¼ cup plain almond butter

2 tablespoons honey

¼ teaspoon ground cinnamon

¼ teaspoon kosher salt

Brioche French Toast
with Peaches and Blueberry Maple Syrup

Serves 4

1½ cups **blueberries**

3 tablespoons **pure cane sugar**

½ cup **maple syrup**

3 large **eggs**

4 large **egg yolks**

1 cup **whole milk**

½ cup **heavy cream**

1 teaspoon **ground cinnamon**

1 tablespoon **pure vanilla extract**

8 slices (¾ inch thick) day-old or stale **brioche bread**

4 to 6 tablespoons **unsalted butter**

2 to 3 teaspoons **neutral oil,** such as avocado or canola

1 large **peach,** sliced into ¼-inch-thick wedges

Powdered sugar, for garnish (optional)

Peaches and blueberries have been one of my favorite combinations since I started cooking. At the peak of summer when both fruits are in season, I'll use them in crisps, cobblers, waffles, even cocktails. Here, I cook the berries until they burst, stir them into a rich maple syrup, and then garnish my French toast with the runny berry syrup and some fresh sliced peaches. The key to success with any French toast is to take the time to really drench the bread in the custard. It should be soaked through.

1. Set an oven rack in the middle position and preheat the oven to 250°F.

2. In a small saucepan, combine the blueberries, 1 tablespoon of the cane sugar, and 1 tablespoon water. Bring to a simmer over medium heat and cook, stirring occasionally, until most of the berries have burst and the juices have released and thickened, 5 to 7 minutes. Stir in the maple syrup and remove from the heat. Cover with a lid and set aside.

3. In a large baking dish, combine the whole eggs, egg yolks, milk, heavy cream, cinnamon, vanilla, and remaining 2 tablespoons cane sugar. Whisk until well combined and smooth. Add half of the bread slices and gently press down until the bread is completely soaked on the first side, about 5 minutes. Flip over and allow to soak on the second side, about 5 minutes. Use a slotted spatula to carefully lift the bread slices out of the custard and transfer to a baking sheet. Repeat the soaking process with the remaining bread.

4. In a large sauté pan, heat 2 tablespoons of the butter and 1 teaspoon of the neutral oil over medium heat until it begins to sizzle. Use a slotted spatula to add 3 or 4 of the soaked bread slices (depending on the size of the bread and your pan) and cook, turning once, until lightly puffed and golden on both sides, 3 to 5 minutes per side. Transfer to a clean baking sheet and place in the oven to keep warm while you cook the remaining French toast. Carefully wipe out the sauté pan after cooking each batch and add fresh butter and oil before adding more bread.

5. Serve the French toast topped with the blueberry maple syrup and scattered with the peach slices. If desired, garnish with a sprinkling of powdered sugar.

Tequila-Cured Salmon

If you're a fan of lox-style salmon, I encourage you to try curing your own—it's actually pretty easy and it's really satisfying. It may take a couple of days to get to round two, but it's worth the wait—especially when one of the steps is breaking out the tequila. When your salmon is ready, you have several options: You could set out bagels, sliced red onions, and cream cheese for a breakfast spread, or you could serve it as a salad—think arugula, white peaches, and some sort of crouton—for a casual lunch.

Please remember to scrape off the spice and salt mixture before serving. One of my most legendary cooking fails was when I forgot to do this during a party at my house in Amagansett. My guests were polite about it, but the salmon was so salty it was pretty much inedible.

1. Line a large sheet pan with a layer of foil and plastic wrap that is large enough to wrap the fish up securely. Lay the salmon onto the lined pan skin side down. Pat the top dry with paper towels.

2. In a small sauté pan, toast the mustard seeds and cumin seeds over medium heat, stirring constantly, until fragrant, 2 to 4 minutes. Transfer to a small bowl to cool slightly, then move to a spice grinder. Add the black peppercorns and coarsely grind.

3. Spread the pureed chipotle onto the flesh of the fish, then sprinkle with the ground spices. Gently press the spices onto the fish. In a small bowl, combine the salt, brown sugar, and ½ cup of the tequila and stir to combine. The mixture will resemble wet sand. Spread it evenly over the salmon, including the sides of the fillet. Drizzle with the remaining ½ cup tequila.

4. Tightly wrap the salmon in the plastic wrap and aluminum foil. Place another baking sheet on top of the salmon and weight it down with cans or a heavy pot or cutting board. Refrigerate until the fish is firm but not dry in texture (it will still have a raw appearance and feel almost leathery), 48 to 72 hours. The curing time will depend on how thick the salmon is; check the fish at 48 hours, then add more time accordingly.

5. Remove the salmon from the refrigerator, drain off the excess liquid, and scrape off the spices and salt mixture. Thinly slice the salmon against the grain and serve. Store any leftovers tightly wrapped in plastic for up to 5 days.

Serves 6 to 8

2-pound skin-on salmon fillet

2 tablespoons yellow mustard seeds

1 tablespoon cumin seeds

1 tablespoon black peppercorns

1 tablespoon pureed canned chipotle pepper in adobo sauce

1½ cups kosher salt

1½ cups packed light brown sugar

1 cup tequila

Banana-Date-Cinnamon Smoothies

Serves 2

1 cup canned **full-fat coconut milk,** well stirred

2 **bananas,** sliced and frozen

2 **Medjool dates,** pitted

1 tablespoon **honey**

1 tablespoon fresh **lime juice**

¼ teaspoon **ground cinnamon,** plus more for garnish

1 cup **ice cubes**

2 **lime wedges,** for garnish

If you make the drive between Los Angeles and Palm Springs you'll almost certainly see a few signs for date shakes, a regional specialty that takes advantage of the fertile crop of California dates. The SoCal date shakes also feature banana, cinnamon (one of my favorite flavors), and ice cream. Here we make it a tad healthier by using coconut milk instead.

In a blender, combine the coconut milk, frozen banana slices, dates, honey, lime juice, cinnamon, and ice cubes. Blend until smooth. Pour into two serving glasses. Sprinkle with additional cinnamon and garnish with the lime wedges.

Scrambled Eggs
with Prosciutto and Focaccia

Serves 4 to 6

Neutral oil, such as avocado or canola, for shallow-frying

8 paper-thin slices **prosciutto**

Freshly ground **black pepper**

12 large **eggs**

4 tablespoons cold **unsalted butter,** cut into small pieces

¼ cup **crème fraîche**

¼ teaspoon **red pepper flakes**

Kosher salt

½ cup freshly grated **Parmigiano-Reggiano cheese,** plus more for garnish

8 pieces **Focaccia** (recipe follows), sliced in half and lightly toasted, for serving

My scrambled eggs have become somewhat of a calling card among my closest friends and family. I used to make them for Sophie and her friends when they were growing up and they were always a hit. During quarantine I really got into baking this focaccia developed by Samin Nosrat for her show *Salt Fat Acid Heat.* Topped with my soft, custardy scrambled eggs, it makes a simple but very satisfying panini. Great for hangovers. (Just a guess.)

1. In a small sauté pan, heat ¼ inch of neutral oil just below medium-high heat until it begins to shimmer. Line a plate with paper towels. Lay 1 slice of prosciutto into the hot oil (be careful of the oil sputtering once the prosciutto is added) and fry until the prosciutto shrinks and becomes almost translucent, 30 seconds to 1 minute per side. Remove the prosciutto to the paper towels and season with black pepper. Continue to fry all the slices, replenishing and reheating the oil as needed. The prosciutto will crisp up as it cools. Set aside while you prepare the eggs.

2. Crack the eggs into a large bowl and whisk until light, frothy, and uniform in color. Strain the eggs through a fine-mesh sieve into a separate bowl.

3. In a large nonstick sauté pan, combine the butter and crème fraîche. Pour the eggs into the pan and add the pepper flakes. Turn the heat to low and cook slowly, mixing frequently and gently using a silicone spatula or a wooden spoon until soft curds form. Depending on the strength of your burner, this can take anywhere from 15 to 35 minutes (sometimes even longer). Remove from the heat (the eggs will still be somewhat wet and have a custard-like consistency). Season with salt and black pepper and gently fold in the Parmigiano.

4. Working quickly so that the eggs do not continue cooking in the hot pan, mound the eggs on top of the warm focaccia and sprinkle with additional Parmigiano-Reggiano and black pepper. Top with the crispy prosciutto and serve as open-faced sandwiches.

Recipe continues

Focaccia

Makes one 18 × 13-inch focaccia

Dough
2½ cups (600g) lukewarm water
½ teaspoon active dry yeast
2½ teaspoons (15g) honey
5⅓ cups (800g) all-purpose flour
2 tablespoons (18g) kosher salt
¼ cup (50g) extra-virgin olive oil, plus more
   for the pan

Brine and finishing
1½ teaspoons (5g) kosher salt
⅓ cup (80g) lukewarm water
Flaky salt
2 to 3 tablespoons extra-virgin olive oil

1. Make the dough: In a medium bowl, stir together the water, yeast, and honey until dissolved. In a very large bowl, whisk together the flour and kosher salt, then add the yeast mixture and olive oil. Stir with a rubber spatula until just incorporated, then scrape the sides of the bowl clean and cover with plastic wrap. Leave out at room temperature until at least doubled in volume, 12 to 14 hours.

2. Spread 2 to 3 tablespoons of olive oil evenly onto an 18 × 13-inch sheet pan. When the dough is ready, use a spatula or your hand to release it from the sides of the bowl and fold it onto itself gently. Pour the dough out onto the pan, then pour an additional 2 tablespoons of olive oil over the dough. Using your hands, gently stretch the dough to the edges of the pan. (The best way to do this is to place your hands underneath the dough mass and pull outward.) The dough will shrink a bit, so repeat stretching once or twice over the course of 30 minutes to ensure that the dough remains spread out over the whole pan.

3. After the dough is stretched, using your fingertips, dimple the dough all over its surface.

4. Make the brine: Stir together the kosher salt and water until the salt is dissolved. Pour the brine over the dough to fill the dimples. Proof the focaccia, uncovered and at room temperature, for 45 minutes, until the dough is light and bubbly.

5. Thirty minutes into this final proof, set one oven rack in the middle position and a second in the top position and preheat the oven to 450°F. If you have a baking stone, place it on the middle rack. Otherwise, invert another sturdy baking sheet and place it on the middle rack. Allow the baking stone or baking sheet to preheat before proceeding with baking.

6. Sprinkle the focaccia with flaky salt. Bake directly on top of the stone or inverted pan until the bottom crust is crisp and golden brown, 25 to 30 minutes. To finish browning the top crust, transfer the focaccia to the upper rack and bake for 5 to 7 minutes longer.

7. Remove the focaccia from the oven and brush the olive oil over the whole surface. Let cool for 5 minutes, then release the focaccia from the pan with a metal spatula and transfer to a wire rack to cool completely.

8. Serve warm or at room temperature. For longer storage, wrap in parchment and keep in an airtight bag or container at room temperature for up to 3 days.

Secret-Weapon Scrambled Eggs

Bobby

I love that my scrambled eggs have a bit of a reputation among Sophie's friends. I'm happy to whip these up any time her crew comes over for breakfast or brunch . . . but I also think they should try making them at home. Scrambled eggs are a great breakfast, lunch, or even dinner option when you're in a hurry and your fridge is looking bare. And they couldn't be easier. All it takes is practice and a little technique.

Start with a cold pan. Scrambled eggs can go from silky and luxurious to rubbery and awful in a matter of seconds. I prefer my scrambled eggs quite soft and custardy, so I start with a cold pan (not chilled, just not on a flame). This helps me control the temperature of the pan and avoid "shocking" the eggs.

Add softened unsalted butter and crème fraîche for richness. Sophie calls crème fraîche my "secret ingredient," but it's not a secret! Crème fraîche is basically cream with some cultures in it. It has that tanginess you'd expect from sour cream, but unlike sour cream, it doesn't split when you heat it. That's why it's crucial in this recipe. I add it to the pan along with the eggs.

Wait to salt. Sprinkle some freshly cracked black pepper as soon as you start cooking your eggs, but hold off on the salt until the very end. If you add salt at the beginning, the salt breaks up the curds.

Pull the pan from the heat while the eggs are still quite soft. Finish stirring away from the flame, then salt as you make your last spin with the spoon. Get the eggs out of the pan and immediately onto the plate. This ensures the cooking process comes to a halt.

Sophie

No one makes better scrambled eggs than my dad. Everyone should strive to make eggs like his! Whenever I had friends over when I was growing up, Dad would make this for our breakfast and it was always such a hit. Now I get texts from my friends: "I'm making your dad's eggs!"

What's funny to me is I would never think to add crème fraîche when I'm making scrambled eggs for myself. Most of the time, I'm eating eggs because I want a protein-rich meal that's on the healthier side. But my dad's scrambled eggs are all about the crème fraîche and butter. As he likes to say, "If I'm going to make myself something, I want it to be as good as it can possibly be. It's not always about being 'healthy.'" The attitude might seem a little old-school, but I love it. And it makes sense! If you're going to take the time to cook something for yourself or others, why not make the most delicious version?

Huevos Rancheros
with Tomato–Red Chile Sauce

Eggs are a big part of breakfast and brunch in our household. I got in the habit of pumping up my standard tomato sauce with chiles and realized it was really versatile. I use it on enchiladas (see Chicken, Mushroom, and Kale Enchilada Casserole, page 97), to liven up roasted vegetables, and here, with eggs and cheesy tostadas. Unfortunately, Sophie is allergic to avocado, so I serve hers with a little sour cream instead.

1. In a small saucepan, heat the olive oil over medium heat. Add the cumin and cook, stirring constantly, until lightly toasted and fragrant, about 30 seconds. Add the black beans and 2 tablespoons water, season with salt and pepper, and cook, stirring occasionally, until warmed through, about 3 minutes. Remove from the heat, cover with a lid, and set aside.

2. In a large nonstick skillet, heat the neutral oil over medium heat until it begins to lightly shimmer. Carefully crack the eggs into the pan, season with salt and pepper, and cook until the whites are completely set but the yolks are still soft, 2 to 4 minutes.

3. Preheat the broiler to high. Place the tostadas on a large baking sheet in a single layer and sprinkle with the Monterey Jack. Broil until the cheese is melted and the tostadas are browned in spots, 1 to 2 minutes.

4. In a small saucepan, warm the tomato-chile sauce over low heat. Place a few spoonfuls of the sauce on each of four plates and set a tostada on top of the sauce. Layer the tostadas with the black beans and fried eggs, then ladle more of the tomato-chile sauce over the top. Top with the avocado and sour cream (if using) and sprinkle with the Cotija and cilantro. Serve immediately with hot sauce.

Serves 4

1 tablespoon extra-virgin olive oil

¼ teaspoon ground cumin

1 (15-ounce) can black beans, drained and rinsed well

Kosher salt and freshly ground black pepper

1 tablespoon neutral oil, such as avocado or canola

4 large eggs

4 tostadas

1 cup coarsely grated Monterey Jack cheese

2 cups Tomato–Red Chile Sauce (page 244)

1 small avocado, diced

⅓ cup sour cream (optional)

⅓ cup crumbled Cotija cheese

Chopped fresh cilantro leaves, for garnish

Hot sauce, for serving

Cacio e Pepe Eggs
with Olive Oil Toast

Serves 4

1½ teaspoons **Dijon mustard**

5 tablespoons **white wine vinegar**

1 teaspoon **honey**

1 small **shallot,** minced

Kosher salt and freshly ground **black pepper**

⅓ cup plus 3 tablespoons **extra-virgin olive oil**

⅓ cup freshly grated **Parmigiano-Reggiano cheese**

8 large **eggs**

4 large slices (½ inch thick) **country loaf**

1 **garlic clove,** halved crosswise

Sliced fresh **chives,** for garnish

I'll never get tired of coming up with new ways to cook and serve eggs. The inspiration here was cacio e pepe, the famous pasta dish of Rome. *Cacio e pepe* translates to "cheese and pepper"—it sounds simple (and it is), but those two ingredients are all it takes to make a phenomenal pasta. In this case, I decided to make a white wine vinaigrette and pump it up with a ton of cheese and black pepper in a nod to cacio e pepe. Of course, I didn't have any Pecorino Romano when I made this, so I used Parmigiano-Reggiano instead. Either works.

1. In a medium bowl, combine the mustard, 3 tablespoons of the vinegar, the honey, shallot, and ½ teaspoon coarsely ground pepper. Season with salt, then whisking briskly, slowly stream in ⅓ cup of the olive oil to emulsify. Whisk in the Parmigiano and set aside.

2. In a large deep sauté pan, combine 6 cups water and the remaining 2 tablespoons vinegar. Bring to a boil over medium-high heat, then reduce to a simmer. Line a plate with paper towels. Break each of 4 of the eggs into an individual cup or small bowl. Use a slotted spoon to swirl the water in the pan to create a small whirlpool, then one at a time gently add an egg in the center. Poach the eggs until the yolk is nearly or almost set, 3 to 5 minutes. Remove the eggs from the pan with a slotted spoon to drain the liquid and place on the paper towels. Season the top with salt and pepper. Repeat with the remaining 4 eggs.

3. Preheat the broiler. Brush the bread slices on both sides with the remaining 3 tablespoons oil and season with salt and pepper. Toast under the broiler until lightly browned and crispy on both sides, 2 to 5 minutes. Rub the toasted bread with the cut sides of the garlic clove.

4. Cut each piece of toast in half crosswise, then top each with a poached egg and drizzle with the dressing. Garnish with sliced chives and serve immediately.

Tacos, Sandwiches, and Handhelds

Quesadillas
with Bacon, Kale, and Monterey Jack

The only thing better than a fully loaded quesadilla is a *double-decker* fully loaded quesadilla. I bake mine, as opposed to the classic technique, which is to fry them. It's a little healthier, still results in a crispy exterior, and makes it easy to cook a bunch at once. Yes, there's bacon and cheese here, but just think about all the benefits you're getting from the addition of kale! So let's pretend they cancel each other out.

1. Make the salsa: In a food processor, combine the tomatoes, jalapeño, garlic, cilantro, honey, vinegar, and olive oil and season with salt and pepper. Pulse until chopped to a chunky consistency. Transfer to a bowl and set aside.

2. Make the quesadillas: Set an oven rack in the middle position and preheat the oven to 400°F.

3. Lay the bacon in a single layer on a sheet pan, leaving ¼ inch between the slices. Bake until lightly browned and crisp, 15 to 25 minutes (depending on the thickness of the bacon). Line a plate with paper towels. Transfer the bacon to the paper towels, let cool slightly, then coarsely chop. Set aside. Carefully drain the fat into a medium bowl (once completely cool, discard). Increase the oven temperature to 450°F.

4. Meanwhile, in a large sauté pan, heat 1 tablespoon of the neutral oil over medium heat. Add the garlic and cook, stirring constantly, until soft, about 30 seconds. Add the kale, season with salt and pepper, and cook, tossing occasionally, until the kale is tender, 6 to 8 minutes. Remove from the heat and set aside.

5. Liberally brush a large baking sheet with neutral oil. Place 4 tortillas on the baking sheet and sprinkle each with ¼ cup of the Monterey Jack. Top evenly with the sautéed kale and season lightly with salt and pepper. Stack another tortilla on top and sprinkle each with another ¼ cup of the cheese. Top evenly with the chopped bacon and chopped cilantro and season lightly with salt and pepper. Top with the remaining 4 tortillas. Brush the top of the tortillas with the remaining 1½ tablespoons oil and sprinkle with the ancho chile powder.

6. Bake until the tortillas are golden brown and crispy and the cheese has completely melted, 5 to 8 minutes. Cut each quesadilla into quarters and transfer to a large platter. Serve immediately alongside the salsa.

Serves 4

Salsa

1 pound **plum tomatoes,** diced

1 **jalapeño,** finely diced

2 **garlic cloves,** finely chopped to a paste with ¼ teaspoon **kosher salt**

3 tablespoons chopped fresh **cilantro leaves**

1 teaspoon **honey**

3 tablespoons **red wine vinegar**

3 tablespoons **extra-virgin olive oil**

Kosher salt and freshly ground **black pepper**

Quesadillas

8 ounces **thick-cut bacon** (about 6 slices)

2½ tablespoons **neutral oil,** such as avocado or canola, plus more for the baking sheet

2 **garlic cloves,** finely chopped to a paste with ¼ teaspoon **kosher salt**

1 bunch **lacinato kale,** ribs and stems removed, leaves coarsely chopped (about 4 cups loosely packed)

Kosher salt and freshly ground **black pepper**

12 (6-inch) **flour tortillas**

2 cups shredded **Monterey Jack cheese**

¼ cup chopped fresh **cilantro leaves**

½ teaspoon **ancho chile powder**

Portobello Mushroom Tacos

Serves 4

1 tablespoon ancho chile powder

1 tablespoon New Mexico chile powder

2 teaspoons ground cumin

4 garlic cloves, finely chopped to a paste with ¼ teaspoon kosher salt

⅓ cup fresh lime juice

½ small red onion, roughly chopped

⅔ cup extra-virgin olive oil

6 portobello mushrooms (about 1½ pounds total), stems discarded

Kosher salt and freshly ground black pepper

8 (6-inch) corn tortillas

Quick-Pickled Red Onions (page 247), for serving

½ cup crumbled goat cheese, for serving

Sliced scallions, for garnish

Chopped fresh cilantro leaves, for garnish

One of my party tricks is I can take pretty much any leftover and turn it into tacos. In this case it was some leftover mushrooms, which I was able to turn into quick-and-easy vegetarian tacos (although you can omit the goat cheese and make them totally vegan, too). The key is to always have an array of taco staples like chiles, limes, onions, garlic, and tortillas in your pantry. That way you're always ready for Taco Night.

1. In a large baking dish, stir together the ancho chile powder, New Mexico chile powder, cumin, garlic, lime juice, red onion, and olive oil. Add the portobello mushroom caps and turn to coat well in the marinade. Cover and refrigerate for at least 30 minutes and up to 8 hours.

2. Set an oven rack in the middle position and preheat the oven to 425°F. Line a large baking sheet with parchment paper and set aside.

3. Transfer the portobello mushrooms to the lined baking sheet, shaking off any excess marinade, and season liberally on both sides with salt and pepper. Roast in the oven, gills side up, until golden brown and tender, about 30 minutes, turning the mushroom caps once halfway through the cooking time. Transfer the mushrooms to a cutting board and allow to cool slightly.

4. Meanwhile, heat a large cast-iron skillet over medium-high heat. Add 1 or 2 tortillas and cook until the tortillas are hot and pliable, 15 to 30 seconds per side. Repeat with the remaining tortillas.

5. Thinly slice the roasted mushroom caps, then divide among the warm corn tortillas, garnish with the quick-pickled red onions, crumbled goat cheese, scallions, and cilantro, and serve.

> ❝
>
> I remember we had guests coming over to our house in Amagansett and one of them was vegan. I think my dad was a little taken aback, because he wanted to make tacos, and up until then all his tacos had some meat component. But he whipped up portobello mushroom tacos, and they were so good. I love to see him dabble with meat-free tacos. —SF
>
> ❞

Tuna Tacos

with Green Papaya Slaw

These tacos remind me of sitting on a beach in San Diego and watching the fishermen bring ahi tuna onto the shore. Local chefs used the fish to make instant poke, tartares, and tacos, just about as fresh as it gets. For my version I hit the tuna with a soy and Fresno chile marinade and then finish the taco with green papaya. It's refreshing and crunchy, which is always a good thing.

1. Make the green papaya slaw: In a large bowl, combine the green papaya, red cabbage, and Fresno chile.

2. In a medium bowl, combine the garlic, shallot, fish sauce, honey, lime juice, and vinegar and season with salt and pepper. Whisk to combine. Pour the dressing over the slaw, season again with salt and pepper, and toss to coat. Let sit for 15 minutes at room temperature. Fold in the mango and cilantro just before serving and season with additional salt and pepper if needed.

3. Make the avocado-corn relish: Set an oven rack in the lowest position and preheat the oven to 425°F.

4. On a small baking sheet, combine the corn kernels and olive oil. Season with salt and pepper and stir to combine, then spread out into a single layer. Roast in the oven until the corn is tender and golden brown in spots, 10 to 15 minutes. Transfer to a bowl to cool.

5. In a medium bowl, mash the avocados until slightly smooth. Gently fold in the cooled roasted corn, sour cream, red onion, serrano (if using), and lime juice and season with salt and pepper. Fold in the cilantro, then set aside until ready to serve.

6. Make the seared tuna: In a small baking dish, combine the Fresno chile, shallot, ginger, garlic, honey, soy sauce, and 2 tablespoons of the neutral oil. Whisk until combined. Add the tuna to the marinade and turn to coat. Cover and refrigerate for at least 30 minutes and up to 1 hour.

Serves 4

Green Papaya Slaw

12 ounces green papaya, peeled and julienned (about 3 cups)

¼ small head red cabbage, shredded

1 Fresno chile, seeded (optional) and finely diced

1 garlic clove, finely chopped to a paste with a pinch of kosher salt

1 small shallot, finely chopped

2 teaspoons fish sauce

1 tablespoon honey

2 tablespoons fresh lime juice

¼ cup rice vinegar

Kosher salt and freshly ground black pepper

1 small firm-ripe mango, peeled and julienned (about 1 cup)

⅓ cup coarsely chopped fresh cilantro leaves

Avocado-Corn Relish

1 ear yellow or white corn, husked and kernels cut from the cob

1 teaspoon extra-virgin olive oil

Kosher salt and freshly ground black pepper

2 large avocados, diced

2 teaspoons sour cream

3 tablespoons finely diced red onion

½ serrano chile, finely diced (optional)

¼ cup fresh lime juice

3 tablespoons finely chopped fresh cilantro leaves

Recipe and ingredients continue

7. Use tongs to transfer the pork to a large bowl, being careful not to break the meat up too much. Skim out any excess fat from the braising liquid, then transfer 1 cup of the liquid to a blender. Remove the steam vent from the center of the lid, cover the small opening with a kitchen towel (this will help to release steam), and blend until smooth.

8. Pour the blended braising liquid back into the Dutch oven, stir to combine, then season with salt and pepper. The sauce should be thick but pourable. If it is too thick, stir in a splash of additional stock or water. Cover with the lid and keep warm over low heat.

9. To serve: In a large cast-iron skillet, heat 1 tablespoon of the neutral oil over medium-high heat until it begins to shimmer. Add half of the braised meat and cook until lightly browned and crispy on the first side, 1 to 2 minutes, lightly pressing down on the pieces of meat to create more crispy edges. Turn the meat and cook until browned and crispy on the second side, 1 to 2 minutes. Transfer the meat to a plate. Add the remaining 1 tablespoon oil and brown the remaining meat.

10. Clean out the cast-iron skillet and heat over medium-high heat. Working with 1 or 2 tortillas at a time, toast the tortillas on both sides until charred in spots, 1 to 2 minutes. Wrap the tortillas in a clean kitchen towel as they come out of the skillet so that they don't dry out.

11. Spoon a thin layer of the braising sauce into the center of each of the warm tortillas, then top with the crispy pork and some of the jicama-cabbage slaw. Garnish with quick-pickled red onions and cilantro leaves and serve immediately with any remaining braising sauce and slaw on the side.

For Serving

2 tablespoons **neutral oil,** such as avocado or canola

8 to 12 (6-inch) **corn tortillas**

Quick-Pickled Red Onions (page 247), for garnish

Fresh **cilantro leaves,** for garnish

Mustardy Lobster Rolls

Lobster rolls easily top the list of "most-consumed foods" Sophie and I eat together as a team! There are several places we love in the Hamptons—Bostwick's being our favorite—so when I don't feel like cooking, we just go there, order two lobster rolls, and surround them with a bowl of steamers and lots of fries. When I'm away from the Hamptons and the lobster roll craving hits, I make them at home. I like to double down on the mustard in the dressing for some real tang.

1. Set up a large container (big enough to hold all the lobsters) of ice and water. Bring a large pot of salted water to a boil. Add the lobsters, cover with a lid, and boil until cooked through, 8 to 10 minutes. Remove the lobsters from the pot and put directly into the ice water bath. Once the lobsters are completely cooled, drain well. Remove the meat from the lobsters and cut into ½-inch chunks (about 2 cups/ 1 pound of meat total).

2. In a large bowl, combine the mustard, mayonnaise, celery, white onion, parsley, and tarragon. Season with salt and pepper. Stir until well combined, then fold in the lobster meat.

3. Brush the insides of the hot dog buns with the melted butter. Heat a large cast-iron skillet over medium heat. Put the buns cut side down into the hot skillet and cook until golden brown and toasted, 2 to 4 minutes.

4. Fill the buns with the lobster salad and arrange on a serving platter. Serve immediately.

Serves 4

Kosher salt

3 (2-pound) whole lobsters

¼ cup whole-grain mustard

⅓ cup mayonnaise

¼ cup finely diced celery

2 tablespoons finely diced white onion

2 tablespoons chopped fresh flat-leaf parsley leaves

1½ teaspoons finely chopped fresh tarragon leaves

Freshly ground black pepper

4 good-quality hot dog buns

3 tablespoons unsalted butter, melted

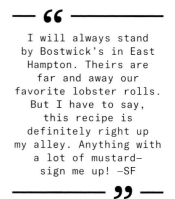

I will always stand by Bostwick's in East Hampton. Theirs are far and away our favorite lobster rolls. But I have to say, this recipe is definitely right up my alley. Anything with a lot of mustard— sign me up! —SF

Meatball Parm Sliders

Makes 12 sliders

A really good red-sauce Italian American joint is Sophie's and my happy place. But sometimes it's hard to commit to a full-size meatball hero—it's a lot of sandwich! That's why I came up with these sliders when I had ground beef and bacon left over from making bacon cheeseburgers the night before. Bonus, they don't require a nap afterward.

1. In a small sauté pan, heat 2 tablespoons of the olive oil over medium heat. Add the garlic and cook, stirring constantly, until soft, about 1 minute. Remove from the heat and let cool slightly.

2. In a large bowl, combine the eggs, sautéed garlic, parsley, and ½ cup of the Parmigiano. Season with salt and pepper and whisk until smooth. Add the bread crumbs and whisk until combined. Add the bacon, ground chuck, and pork and use your hands to mix until combined. Cover and refrigerate for at least 1 hour and up to 8 hours.

3. Form the meat into 1½-inch balls. You should get about 12 total. Line a baking sheet with paper towels.

4. In a large deep sauté pan, heat the remaining ¾ cup oil over medium-high heat until it begins to shimmer. Add the meatballs and fry until golden brown on all sides, about 8 minutes. Using a slotted spoon, carefully transfer the meatballs to the paper towels to drain.

5. Remove the pan from the heat and carefully pour the used oil into a heatproof bowl (once cooled, discard the oil). Pour the tomato sauce into the sauté pan and heat over medium heat until the sauce starts to simmer, 3 to 5 minutes, scraping up any browned bits at the bottom of the pan. Season with salt and pepper, add the meatballs, turn to coat in the sauce, reduce the heat to low, and simmer for 20 minutes.

6. Preheat the broiler. Arrange the slider buns on a large baking sheet, cut side up. Toast under the broiler until lightly browned and crusty, 1 to 2 minutes. Remove the top buns to a plate. On each of the bottom buns, spread a spoonful of sauce, add 1 meatball, and top with a slice of mozzarella. Sprinkle with the remaining ¼ cup Parmigiano, then return to the broiler and broil until the mozzarella is melted and lightly browned in spots, 2 to 4 minutes.

7. Transfer to a large platter, top with the baby arugula, and add the top buns. Serve immediately with any remaining tomato sauce on the side.

¾ cup plus 2 tablespoons extra-virgin olive oil

4 garlic cloves, finely chopped to a paste with ¼ teaspoon kosher salt

2 large eggs

¼ cup finely chopped fresh flat-leaf parsley leaves

¾ cup freshly grated Parmigiano-Reggiano cheese

Kosher salt and freshly ground black pepper

¼ cup plain dried bread crumbs

4 ounces thick-cut bacon (about 3 slices), finely chopped (about ½ cup packed)

½ pound ground chuck (80% lean)

½ pound ground pork

4 cups Basic Tomato Sauce (page 243)

12 crusty sourdough dinner rolls (about 2½ inches across), split apart

12 slices (⅛ inch thick) fresh mozzarella cheese

¾ cup lightly packed baby arugula (about ¾ ounce)

Ballpark Hot Italian Sausages
with Caramelized Onions

These spicy pork sausages, seared in a cast-iron pan or on a hot grill until they're deeply browned and have a crackly crust, remind me of going to a game at Yankee Stadium. Who doesn't love ballpark cuisine at home? I go for spicy sausages instead of hot dogs because I want that extra texture and that extra heat (which I take even further by adding a few Fresno chiles). If you've never caramelized onions before, the key is to let them go for a while—longer than you might think. Your patience will be rewarded with sweet, meltingly tender onions. I'm not really a big beer fan, but in this case nothing could be more appropriate.

1. In a large cast-iron skillet, heat 2 tablespoons of the neutral oil over medium-high heat until it begins to shimmer. Add the onions and stir to coat in the oil. Add the sugar and season with salt and pepper. Cook the onions, stirring frequently, until softened and starting to brown in spots, about 10 minutes. Reduce the heat to medium, add the butter and chiles (more or less depending on how spicy you want it), and continue cooking, stirring occasionally, until the onions are golden brown and caramelized, 25 to 35 minutes. Transfer the onions and chiles to a bowl and set aside.

2. Add the remaining 1 tablespoon oil to the skillet and place the sausages cut side down. Cook on medium heat until deeply browned and crusty on the first side, 2 to 3 minutes. Flip and cook until browned on the second side and the sausages are cooked through, about 2 minutes longer.

3. Slather the split rolls with mustard and layer with the caramelized onions and sausages. Serve immediately.

Serves 4

3 tablespoons **neutral oil,** such as avocado or canola

2 large **Spanish onions,** halved and thinly sliced (about 6 cups)

1 teaspoon **sugar**

Kosher salt and freshly ground **black pepper**

1 tablespoon **unsalted butter**

1 to 2 **Fresno chiles,** to taste, thinly sliced

4 **hot Italian sausages,** split lengthwise

4 crusty **hoagie rolls,** split and toasted

Hot and/or sweet German mustard, for serving

Crunch Burgers

with BBQ Mushrooms

Serves 4

4 tablespoons **neutral oil,** such as avocado or canola

1 pound **cremini mushrooms,** thinly sliced (about 8 cups)

⅔ cup **barbecue sauce,** homemade (page 248) or store-bought

Kosher salt and freshly ground **black pepper**

1½ pounds **ground chuck** (80% lean)

8 slices **American cheese**

4 **potato hamburger buns,** split and toasted

⅓ cup **Quick-Pickled Red Onions** (page 247)

4 handfuls of **potato chips**

Just when I thought my signature crunch burger couldn't get any better, barbecue mushrooms take the stage. The combo of umami-rich mushrooms and fiery barbecue sauce makes this taste like a smokehouse burger, no smoker required. I created this burger at home, but I liked it so much I decided to add it to the menu at my restaurant Bobby's Burgers.

1. In a large cast-iron skillet, heat 2 tablespoons of the neutral oil over medium-high heat until it begins to shimmer. Add the mushrooms and cook until browned and tender, stirring occasionally, about 15 minutes. Reduce the heat to low, stir in the barbecue sauce, and season with salt and pepper. Cook until the sauce becomes sticky and coats the mushrooms, stirring constantly, 1 to 2 minutes. Transfer to a bowl and set aside.

2. Divide the meat into 4 equal portions (6 ounces each). Form each portion loosely into a burger ¾ inch thick and make a deep depression in the center with your thumb. Season both sides of each burger with salt and pepper.

3. Clean out the cast-iron skillet you used for the mushrooms and heat the remaining 2 tablespoons oil over high heat until it begins to shimmer. Cook the burgers until golden brown and slightly charred on the first side, about 3 minutes.

4. Flip the burgers over. Cook until golden brown and slightly charred on the second side, about 3 minutes for medium-rare, or until cooked to your desired degree of doneness. Add the cheese and the mushrooms to the tops of the burgers during the last minute of cooking and top with a lid until the cheese is melted, about 1 minute.

5. Place the burgers on the bun bottoms and top with the pickled red onions. Pile on the potato chips, top with the bun tops, and serve immediately.

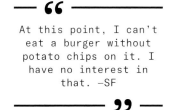

> At this point, I can't eat a burger without potato chips on it. I have no interest in that. —SF

Open-Faced Lemon and Garlic Marinated Steak Sandwiches

with Triple-Crème Cheese

Serves 4

Finely grated zest and juice
    of 1 small lemon (about
    2 tablespoons juice)

3 garlic cloves, finely
    chopped to a paste with
    ¼ teaspoon kosher salt

2 teaspoons chopped fresh
    thyme leaves

1 tablespoon chopped fresh
    oregano leaves

¼ cup plus 2 tablespoons
    extra-virgin olive oil

1½ pounds skirt steak,
    cut crosswise into
    3 or 4 pieces

Kosher salt and freshly
    ground black pepper

4 slices (½ inch thick)
    ciabatta bread, cut
    across the loaf on the
    diagonal

8 ounces triple-crème
    cheese, rind removed, at
    room temperature

1½ cups lightly packed baby
    arugula (about 1 ounce)

Skirt steak is an underrated cut, but I love it because it has so much beefy flavor. Here, I wanted to give it the sandwich treatment, but I decided not to cover the steak with a piece of toast on top. Think of it as an Italian-style crostino. You could cut it into quarters and serve it with some cocktails as aperitivo or leave it whole and serve it as a main. A soft, buttery triple-crème cheese like Saint André or Cowgirl Creamery's Mt Tam will make anything taste good.

1. In a large baking dish, combine the lemon zest and juice, garlic, thyme, oregano, and ¼ cup of the olive oil. Stir to mix, then add the steaks and turn to coat in the marinade. Cover and refrigerate for at least 1 hour and up to 2 hours.

2. Remove the steaks from the refrigerator 30 minutes before cooking, to take the chill off. If cooking outdoors, preheat a charcoal or gas grill to high heat. If cooking indoors, heat a large cast-iron skillet or grill pan over high heat until it is screaming hot, and open some windows—it's about to get smoky!

3. Season the steaks on both sides with salt and pepper. Grill or sear until charred on both sides and cooked to medium-rare, 2 to 4 minutes per side. Transfer to a cutting board to rest for 5 minutes.

4. Meanwhile, brush the bread slices on one side with the remaining 2 tablespoons oil and season with salt. Grill or toast on both sides until charred in spots, 1 to 2 minutes per side. Remove from the heat and immediately slather the oil-toasted side with the triple-crème cheese.

5. Thinly slice the steaks against the grain. On a large platter or four individual plates, place the toasts and top with the sliced steak and baby arugula. Serve immediately.

Old-School Chicken Salad

Serves 4

¾ cup **mayonnaise**

2 teaspoons **red wine vinegar**

1 heaping tablespoon **Dijon mustard**

½ small **red onion**, finely diced

1 medium **celery stalk**, finely diced

2 tablespoons finely chopped **cornichons** (capers are a nice alternative here)

½ teaspoon chopped fresh **tarragon leaves**

4 cups chopped or shredded cooked **chicken** (about 1 pound)

Kosher salt and freshly ground **black pepper**

8 slices **Pullman-style bread,** toasted until lightly golden

8 **romaine** or **iceberg lettuce leaves**

Lately when Sophie comes over, she's been making a beeline for the fridge to scour the shelves for my homemade chicken salad. This is a relatively new phenomenon, but I'm happy to oblige her. Whenever I make chicken soup (page 119), I take any leftover chicken (which tends to be pretty well cooked) and bring it back to life with plenty of mayo and crisp chopped vegetables. I serve this chicken salad in lettuce wraps, in a classic sandwich, or sometimes just as an open-faced crostino.

1. In a medium bowl, combine the mayonnaise, vinegar, and mustard. Whisk to combine, then stir in the red onion, celery, cornichons, and tarragon. Gently fold in the chicken. Season with salt and pepper.

2. Divide among 4 slices of toast, top with the lettuce leaves, then the remaining toast. Slice each sandwich in half and serve.

Variation

You can also serve this chicken salad on focaccia or a hamburger bun, spread on crunchy lettuce or radicchio leaves (Treviso is a favorite), in a tomato, or just eat it with a fork out of the bowl you made it in.

> I became so obsessed with chicken salad sandwiches during quarantine, I practically begged my dad to make them. In my freezer, I still have quarts of the chicken soup he'd make specifically so he'd have leftovers for my chicken salad. I never got sick of it. Him . . . I think maybe *he* got a little sick of it. —SF

Pasta, Rice, and Polenta

Shrimp Mafaldine

with Saffron, Anchovy, and Calabrian Chile

Serves 4 to 6

Kosher salt

1 pound dried mafaldine pasta

4 tablespoons extra-virgin olive oil

1 pound large shrimp (21/25 count), peeled and deveined (shells reserved for stock), tail off

Freshly ground black pepper

4 garlic cloves, finely chopped to a paste with ¼ teaspoon kosher salt

½ teaspoon red pepper flakes (preferably Calabrian)

1 oil-packed anchovy fillet, drained and finely chopped

1 cup Shrimp Stock (page 243), plus more as needed

Pinch of saffron

3 tablespoons unsalted butter, cut into pieces

½ cup freshly grated Parmigiano-Reggiano cheese, plus more for garnish

Finely grated zest and juice of 1 lemon

2 tablespoons chopped fresh flat-leaf parsley leaves

2 tablespoons chopped fresh basil leaves, plus more for garnish

This pasta may be the most requested dish among my friends, Sophie included. When I hear cries of "Make the shrimp pasta," I know peeling lots of shrimp is in my near future. But that's the key to making this dish special: buying shell-on shrimp, peeling and deveining them yourself, and making your own concentrated stock (see Shrimp Stock, page 243) with the shrimp shells. It's better than anything you can find at the store. Mafaldine are wide pasta ribbons with crinkly edges that help catch all the delicious sauce. If you can't find it, try pappardelle or fettuccine instead.

1. Bring a large pot of water to a boil over high heat. Season the water generously with salt. Add the pasta to the water and cook for 2 minutes less than directed on the package. Drain well.

2. Meanwhile, in a large deep sauté pan, heat 3 tablespoons of the olive oil over medium-high heat until it begins to shimmer. Season the shrimp on both sides with salt and black pepper. Add the shrimp to the pan in an even layer and sear until just opaque and golden on both sides, but not cooked through, about 2 minutes. Transfer the shrimp to a plate.

3. Add the remaining 1 tablespoon oil to the pan and heat until it begins to shimmer. Add the garlic, pepper flakes, and anchovy fillet and cook until fragrant, about 30 seconds. Add the shrimp stock and saffron, increase the heat to high, and scrape any browned bits to incorporate. Cook until the stock is reduced by half, 2 to 4 minutes. Add the shrimp and any juices that collected on the plate back to the pan and let simmer, stirring occasionally, until the shrimp are opaque throughout, about 1 minute.

4. Reduce the heat to medium and add the drained pasta to the pan along with the butter, Parmigiano, half of the lemon zest, and all the lemon juice. Toss to coat and combine, adding additional stock to loosen up the sauce if needed. Season with salt and black pepper. Fold in the parsley and basil and transfer to a large serving platter.

5. Garnish with the remaining lemon zest and additional Parmigiano and basil. Serve immediately.

Elevate Your Pasta Game

Sophie

For me, this pasta epitomizes summer at my dad's house. We're all sitting at his table on Long Island, but in his mind, he's off on the Amalfi Coast of Italy. This pasta is his way of transporting everyone else to where he is, one of his favorite places on Earth. He makes a huge batch to feed the crowd of people who always seem to wander over for lunch, and there are always leftovers—which is great, because I find myself craving shrimp pasta for the rest of the weekend. His goal may have been to send us on a taste journey to Italy, but when I eat this, I'm transported to *my* happy place: the Amagansett house, surrounded by friends and family on a beautiful summer day.

Bobby

Pasta is definitely one of my love languages. It's what I cook to make people feel happy and at home. But knowing how to cook pasta is also one of those foundational techniques that every beginner cook should know. Pasta is such a great and economical way to feed yourself. If you always have dried pasta and a few accoutrements (anchovy, chile peppers, garlic, and salty cheeses like Pecorino Romano and Parmigiano) in your pantry, you'll never go hungry.

I think a lot of people assume pasta is an easy, throwaway dish—"it's just pasta." It's true that pasta can be a really quick meal because the cooking times are short. In some cases, you can have a meal ready in basically the amount of time it takes to bring a pot of water to a boil. But there's a difference between making a good pasta and a great one. All it takes is a few key steps.

Salt the water you're cooking the pasta in so it tastes like the ocean. The key to well-seasoned pasta is well-seasoned water.

Pull your pasta from the boiling water a minute or two before it's tender. This is usually a minute or two before the lower range on the package directions. Transfer it directly to the sauce and finish cooking it there.

Don't dump all the pasta water! Save some of it in case you need to adjust your sauce's consistency. (It'll probably be too thick and need to get thinned out a bit.) The starchy pasta water has the added benefit of helping bind the pasta and the sauce. That's how you get the sauce to coat each individual strand of pasta.

Go green. Add freshly chopped green herbs at the very end, before you plate it.

Don't be afraid to season aggressively. Salty cheeses, briny anchovies, and red pepper flakes are your friends.

Mussels and Squid Fettuccine

Serves 4 to 6

Mussels and the broth they create is one of my all-time favorite flavors. I always feel like squid doesn't get its due, unless it's encased in fried batter. So here I simmer the squid, which gives you fantastic texture and a stunning purple color.

1. Bring a large pot of salted water to a boil. Add the pasta to the water and cook for 2 minutes less than directed on the package. Reserving 1 cup of the pasta water, drain the pasta. Set the pasta and pasta water aside.

2. In a large deep sauté pan, heat the olive oil over medium-high heat until it starts to shimmer. Add the shallot, season with salt and black pepper, and cook until soft, stirring frequently, about 3 minutes. Add half of the garlic and cook until soft, about 30 seconds. Stir in the mussels, add the wine, and immediately cover the pan. Cook until the mussels are opened, 3 to 5 minutes.

3. Remove from the heat and use a slotted spoon to transfer the mussels to a large bowl. (Discard any mussels that have not opened.) Allow the mussels to cool slightly, then carefully remove the meat from the shells and pour any extra mussel liquor back into the pan. Put the meat in a separate bowl and set aside; discard the shells.

4. Turn the heat under the pan back to medium-high and bring the cooking liquid to a boil. Reduce the heat to medium-low for a strong simmer and cook until reduced by half, about 10 minutes. Add the remaining garlic, the anchovies, oregano, and pepper flakes and cook for 1 minute. Add the squid, season with salt and black pepper, and cook for 1 minute (they will not be cooked through at this point). Add the tomato puree and cook, stirring constantly, for 2 minutes, adjusting the heat as needed to maintain an active simmer.

5. Stir in the cold butter, piece by piece, until the sauce is slightly thickened and creamy. Stir in the cooked mussels, then add the cooked pasta and toss to coat and combine. Add a few splashes of reserved pasta water as needed to ensure the sauce coats the pasta and to reach your desired consistency. Fold in the parsley, slivered basil, and lemon zest and season with salt and black pepper.

6. Transfer the pasta to a large shallow serving bowl. Sprinkle with the toasted garlic-lemon bread crumbs (if using) and garnish with parsley, basil, and lemon zest. Drizzle with some oil and serve immediately.

Kosher salt

1 pound dried fettuccine

3 tablespoons extra-virgin olive oil, plus more for drizzling

1 shallot, finely diced

Freshly ground black pepper

4 garlic cloves, finely chopped with ¼ teaspoon kosher salt

2 pounds mussels, scrubbed and debearded

1 cup dry white wine

2 oil-packed anchovy fillets, drained and finely chopped

2 teaspoons chopped fresh oregano leaves

½ teaspoon red pepper flakes

12 ounces squid (bodies and tentacles), cleaned, bodies sliced into rings ¼ inch wide

1 cup tomato puree

3 tablespoons cold unsalted butter, cut into tablespoons

2 tablespoons chopped fresh flat-leaf parsley leaves, plus more for garnish

10 fresh basil leaves, tightly rolled and thinly sliced, plus hand-torn leaves for garnish

Finely grated zest of 1 lemon, plus more for garnish

¼ cup Toasted Garlic-Lemon Bread Crumbs (optional; page 248)

Creamy Rigatoni
with Spicy Sausage and Eggplant

I always cook more sausages than I'm going to eat because I want the effort to last for a few days. Sausage for eggs or an omelet, sausage on a pizza or in a tortilla . . . leftover sausage is the gift that keeps giving. One of my favorite moves is to use it in a pasta sauce. Rigatoni and sausage have been good friends for a really long time, and this bowl of deliciousness proves it.

1. Set an oven rack in the middle position and preheat the oven to 425°F.

2. Place the eggplant on a large baking sheet, drizzle with ¼ cup of the olive oil, and season with salt and pepper. Spread out the eggplant into a single layer and roast until golden brown and tender, about 30 minutes.

3. Meanwhile, bring a large pot of water to a boil over high heat. Season the water generously with salt. Add the pasta to the water and cook for 2 minutes less than directed on the package, 7 to 9 minutes. Reserving 1 cup of pasta water, drain the pasta well. Set the pasta and pasta water aside.

4. Meanwhile, in a large deep sauté pan, heat the remaining 2 tablespoons oil over medium-high heat until it begins to shimmer. Add the sausages in an even layer and sear until browned on both sides and just cooked through, about 2 minutes. Using a slotted spoon, transfer the sausage to a plate.

5. Add the wine to the pan and cook until reduced by half, about 2 minutes, scraping up any browned bits at the bottom of the pan. Add the tomato sauce, season with salt and pepper, and cook for 5 minutes. Stir in the sausage and roasted eggplant and let simmer for 2 minutes, stirring occasionally.

6. Reduce the heat to medium and add the drained pasta and crème fraîche to the pan. Toss to coat and combine. Add a few splashes of reserved pasta water as needed to ensure the sauce coats the pasta and to reach your desired consistency. Season with salt and pepper. Fold in the oregano and basil and transfer to a large serving platter.

7. Garnish with additional basil and serve immediately.

Serves 4

1 large **eggplant** (about 1 pound), peeled and cut into ¾-inch cubes

¼ cup plus 2 tablespoons **extra-virgin olive oil**

Kosher salt and freshly ground **black pepper**

1 pound **dried rigatoni**

3 **hot Italian sausages,** cut crosswise into coins ½ inch thick

½ cup **dry red wine**

3 cups **Basic Tomato Sauce** (page 243)

½ cup **crème fraîche**

2 teaspoons chopped fresh **oregano leaves**

3 tablespoons chopped fresh **basil leaves,** plus more for garnish

Orecchiette

with Ricotta, Asparagus, and Golden Tomatoes

The first time I made this dish was for an Easter brunch in Los Angeles. I bought bright and beautiful asparagus and yellow Sungold tomatoes from the farmers' market in Hollywood. Don't skip the lemony bread crumbs. Their crunchy texture makes the dish.

1. Bring a large pot of water to a boil over high heat. Season the water generously with salt. Add the pasta to the water and cook for 2 minutes less than directed on the package. Reserving 1 cup of the pasta water, drain the pasta well. Set the pasta and pasta water aside.

2. Meanwhile, in a small bowl, combine the ricotta and chives and season with salt and black pepper. Stir to combine and set aside.

3. Rub the asparagus with 3 tablespoons of the olive oil and season with salt and black pepper. Place in a large deep sauté pan and turn the heat to high. Cook, without stirring, until the asparagus is bright green and crisp-tender, 3 to 4 minutes. Transfer the asparagus to a large plate and set aside.

4. Reduce the heat under the pan to medium-high and add the remaining 3 tablespoons oil. Add the shallot, garlic, and pepper flakes and cook, stirring constantly, for 2 minutes.

5. Add the tomatoes and season with salt and black pepper. Cook, stirring occasionally, until the tomatoes start to break down but still hold their shape, about 2 minutes. Add half of the reserved pasta water and cook until the liquid is reduced by half, about 2 minutes.

6. Add the lemon zest, lemon juice, butter, and Parmigiano and stir until combined and creamy. Add the drained pasta and cooked asparagus. Toss to coat and combine. Add a few splashes of reserved pasta water as needed to ensure the sauce coats the pasta and to reach your desired consistency. Fold in the slivered basil and season with salt and black pepper.

7. Transfer to a large serving platter. Sprinkle the pasta with the bread crumbs and additional Parmigiano. Dollop the chive-ricotta on top and garnish with the hand-torn basil. Drizzle with some oil and serve immediately.

Serves 4

Kosher salt

12 ounces **dried orecchiette pasta**

½ cup **whole-milk ricotta cheese**

1 tablespoon sliced fresh **chives**

Freshly ground **black pepper**

1 pound **asparagus,** trimmed and sliced on a slight diagonal into ½-inch pieces

6 tablespoons **extra-virgin olive oil,** plus more for drizzling

1 large **shallot,** thinly sliced

4 **garlic cloves,** finely chopped to a paste with ¼ teaspoon **kosher salt**

¼ teaspoon **red pepper flakes**

1 pound **yellow cherry tomatoes** (about 4 cups), halved

Finely grated zest and juice of 1 **lemon**

2 tablespoons cold **unsalted butter,** cut into small pieces

½ cup freshly grated **Parmigiano-Reggiano cheese,** plus more for garnish

10 fresh **basil leaves,** tightly rolled and thinly sliced, plus hand-torn leaves for garnish

½ cup **Toasted Garlic-Lemon Bread Crumbs** (page 248)

Spaghetti

with Zucchini and Shishito Pesto

Serves 4 to 6

Kosher salt

1 pound **dried spaghetti**

Neutral oil, such as avocado or canola, for shallow-frying

2 medium **zucchini,** scrubbed and thinly sliced into coins

Freshly ground **black pepper**

2 tablespoons **extra-virgin olive oil,** plus more for drizzling

3 **garlic cloves,** finely chopped to a paste with ¼ teaspoon **kosher salt**

4 tablespoons **unsalted butter,** cut into pieces

⅓ cup **Shishito Pesto** (page 244)

½ cup freshly grated **Parmigiano-Reggiano cheese,** plus more for garnish

10 fresh **basil leaves,** tightly rolled and thinly sliced, plus hand-torn leaves for garnish

This dish is very special and means a lot to me. The first time I had zucchini pasta was at my favorite place to eat lunch, probably anywhere in the world, the restaurant Lo Scoglio on the Amalfi Coast. The chef, Tomasso, showed me how to make his version, which is known in that region as *spaghetti alla nerano.* I, of course, had to put my own spin on it by adding pesto with shishito peppers. This dish made it onto my menu at Amalfi in Vegas. It's an instant classic.

1. Bring a large pot of water to a boil and season generously with salt. Add the pasta to the water and cook for 2 minutes less than directed on the package. Reserving 1½ cups of the pasta water, drain the pasta well. Set the pasta and pasta water aside.

2. Meanwhile, in a large deep sauté pan, heat ½ inch of neutral oil over medium-high heat until it shimmers. Line a plate with paper towels. Add the zucchini to the pan and cook, stirring occasionally, until golden brown and toasted, 8 to 12 minutes. (This takes awhile since zucchini's high-water content needs to cook out before it will brown.) Use a slotted spoon to transfer the zucchini to the paper towels to drain. Season with salt and pepper and set aside. Remove the pan from the heat and carefully pour the used oil into a heatproof bowl (once cooled discard the oil).

3. Return the sauté pan to medium heat and add the olive oil. Add the garlic and cook until soft, about 1 minute. (Do not let the garlic overcook or achieve any color.) Add the browned zucchini, ½ cup of the reserved pasta water, and the butter. Stir until well combined and creamy, 1 to 2 minutes.

4. Increase the heat to medium-high, add the pasta and a splash of the reserved pasta water, and toss to coat. Add the shishito pesto and Parmigiano and stir to combine. Continue to cook until just combined, about 30 seconds. Add a few more splashes of reserved pasta water as needed to ensure the sauce coats the pasta and to reach your desired consistency. Remove from the heat and fold in the slivered basil.

5. Transfer the pasta to a large platter. Drizzle with some olive oil and sprinkle with Parmigiano and the hand-torn basil and serve.

Linguine
with Cherry Tomatoes and Anchovies

This is one of my favorite summertime pastas because unlike a stewed tomato sauce, you don't have to prep this hours ahead of time. All season long, I buy tons of cherry tomatoes from a farm stand in Amagansett called Balsam Farms. When they're a bit past their prime and start to soften, I toss them in a pan with olive oil, crushed anchovies, and garlic for an instant sauce. It's light but still crazy flavorful.

1. Bring a large pot of water to a boil. Season the water generously with salt. Add the pasta to the water and cook for 2 minutes less than the package directions. Reserving 1 cup of the pasta water, drain the pasta well. Set the pasta and pasta water aside.

2. Meanwhile, in a large deep sauté pan, heat the olive oil over medium heat until it begins to shimmer. Add the garlic and cook, stirring constantly, until fragrant, about 1 minute. Stir in the pepper flakes and anchovies and cook until the anchovies melt into the oil, about 2 minutes.

3. Increase the heat to high, add the cherry tomatoes, and cook until some of the tomatoes just start to soften, about 2 minutes.

4. Add the butter, 1 tablespoon at a time, stirring until the butter is creamy and incorporated into the sauce. Add the pasta and toss with tongs to coat. Add a few splashes of reserved pasta water, if needed, to ensure that the pasta is well coated with the sauce and to achieve your desired consistency. Stir in the basil and season with salt and black pepper.

5. Transfer to a shallow serving bowl or divide among individual bowls and garnish with additional basil and the grated Parmigiano. Serve immediately.

Serves 4 to 6

Kosher salt

1 pound **dried linguine**

¼ cup **extra-virgin olive oil**

6 **garlic cloves,** finely chopped to a paste with ½ teaspoon **kosher salt**

¼ teaspoon **red pepper flakes**

6 oil-packed **anchovy fillets,** drained and finely chopped

1 pound **cherry tomatoes** (about 4 cups), halved

3 tablespoons cold **unsalted butter,** cut into tablespoons

¼ cup hand-torn fresh **basil,** plus more for garnish

Freshly ground **black pepper**

Freshly grated **Parmigiano-Reggiano cheese,** for garnish

Shiitake Mushroom Penne
with Arugula

Serves 4 to 6

Kosher salt

1 pound **dried penne rigate pasta**

⅓ cup **extra-virgin olive oil,** plus more for drizzling

4 oil-packed **anchovy fillets,** drained and finely chopped

1 pound **shiitake mushrooms,** stems discarded, caps thinly sliced (about 10 cups)

Freshly ground **black pepper**

4 **garlic cloves,** finely chopped to a paste with ¼ teaspoon salt

½ cup **dry white wine**

2 tablespoons **unsalted butter**

¾ cup freshly grated **Pecorino Romano cheese,** plus more for garnish

1 cup lightly packed **baby arugula** (about 1 ounce), plus more for garnish

This is another family-style meal that came to fruition when I went through my refrigerator, found what seemed like a good combination of flavors, and decided to wrap them around some penne, one of the many shapes of dried pasta I keep in my pantry. As always, anchovy is the ingredient that elevates this dish from good to very good!

1. Bring a large pot of water to a boil. Season the water generously with salt. Add the pasta to the water and cook for 2 minutes less than directed on the package. Reserving 1½ cups of the pasta water, drain the pasta well. Set the pasta and pasta water aside.

2. In a large deep sauté pan, heat the olive oil over medium heat. Add the anchovies and cook, stirring constantly, until the anchovies melt into the oil, 1 to 2 minutes.

3. Increase the heat to medium-high and add the shiitake mushrooms. Season with salt and pepper and cook, stirring frequently, until golden brown and tender, 12 to 15 minutes. Add the garlic and cook, stirring constantly, until soft, about 1 minute. Add the wine and cook until almost completely dry, about 1 minute, scraping up any browned bits at the bottom of the pan.

4. Reduce the heat to medium and add the pasta, butter, and Romano and stir until the butter and cheese are completely melted. Stir in the reserved pasta water as needed to ensure that the pasta is coated in the light sauce and to achieve your desired consistency. Season with salt and pepper. Remove from the heat and stir in the baby arugula.

5. Transfer to a large serving bowl, top with more arugula, and drizzle with some oil. Sprinkle with some Romano and serve immediately.

Classic Spaghetti and Meatballs

Very few dishes get me and Sophie more excited than this Italian American classic. You're probably not going to see spaghetti and meatballs together in the same bowl in a good trattoria in Rome, but when it comes to Sunday dinner at my house, this bowl of red sauce and noodles topped with rich, flavorful meatballs is always welcome. I make garlic bread by toasting Italian bread in the oven and slathering it all over with fresh garlic butter. That and a *Sopranos* rerun are the perfect accompaniment.

Note: *I find that most store-bought ricotta does not need to be drained before using in this recipe. However, if you find that yours is especially milky, let it drain in a colander lined with cheesecloth or a coffee filter (weighted with a plate if needed) for at least 1 hour. You can also use 1 to 2 extra tablespoons of bread crumbs to help absorb the excess liquid.*

1. Make the meatballs: In a small sauté pan, heat 2 tablespoons of the olive oil over medium heat. Add the garlic and cook, stirring constantly, until soft, about 1 minute. Remove from the heat and let cool slightly.

2. In a large bowl, combine the egg, sautéed garlic, ricotta, parsley, and Parmigiano and season with salt and pepper. Whisk until smooth. Add the bread crumbs and whisk until combined. Add the ground chuck and pork and use your hands to mix them together until combined. Cover and refrigerate for at least 1 hour and up to 8 hours. The longer you let the mixture chill, the more the flavor develops and the better the meatballs will stay together during frying.

3. Form the meat into 1½-inch balls, about 12 total. In a large sauté pan, heat the remaining ¾ cup oil over medium-high heat until it begins to shimmer. Line a baking sheet with paper towels. Add the meatballs and fry until golden brown on all sides, about 8 minutes. Using a slotted spoon, carefully transfer the meatballs to the paper towels to drain. Remove the pan from the heat and carefully pour the used oil into a heatproof bowl (once cooled, discard the oil). Set the pan aside to use when saucing the pasta.

Recipe continues

Serves 4 to 6

Meatballs

¾ cup plus 2 tablespoons **extra-virgin olive oil**

4 **garlic cloves,** finely chopped to a paste with ¼ teaspoon **kosher salt**

1 large **egg**

⅓ cup **whole-milk ricotta cheese** (see Note)

¼ cup finely chopped fresh **flat-leaf parsley leaves**

½ cup freshly grated **Parmigiano-Reggiano cheese**

Kosher salt and freshly ground **black pepper**

¼ cup **plain dried bread crumbs**

½ pound **ground chuck** (80% lean)

½ pound **ground pork**

Basic Tomato Sauce (page 243)

Spaghetti

Kosher salt

1 pound **dried spaghetti**

2 tablespoons **unsalted butter**

¼ cup freshly grated **Parmigiano-Reggiano cheese,** plus more for garnish

Hand-torn fresh **basil leaves,** for garnish

4. In a large deep sauté pan or Dutch oven, heat the tomato sauce over medium heat until it starts to simmer, about 5 minutes. Season with salt and pepper and add the meatballs. Reduce the heat to low and simmer until the meatballs are cooked through, about 15 minutes.

5. Meanwhile, cook the spaghetti: Bring a large pot of water to a boil over high heat. Season the water generously with salt. Add the pasta to the water and cook for 2 minutes less than directed on the package. Reserving 1 cup of the pasta water, drain the pasta well. Set the pasta and pasta water aside.

6. Wipe out the sauté pan used to panfry the meatballs and add a few large ladles of the tomato sauce (about 3 cups). Heat over medium-high heat until the sauce starts to simmer, 1 to 2 minutes. Add the drained pasta, the butter, and Parmigiano. Use tongs to coat the pasta in the sauce. Add more sauce and a few splashes of reserved pasta water as needed to ensure the sauce coats each strand of pasta and to reach your desired consistency.

7. Transfer the spaghetti to a platter or large shallow bowl and top with the meatballs. Ladle some of the remaining sauce over the spaghetti and meatballs. Garnish with lots of Parmigiano and basil and serve.

Crispy Rice, Two Ways

Crispy rice is one of my weapons (and it's not a secret). If you've seen *Beat Bobby Flay* you've probably seen me crisp up the rice component on one of my dishes. The judges always like it and my harshest critic, Sophie Flay, likes it, too. Crispy rice for the win, every time. Not only does it go with everything—saucy curries or braises, grilled meats, you name it—but it's also a great way to use up leftover rice. If you're starting from scratch with fresh rice, be sure to let it cool completely before you crisp it up.

Crispy Rice
with Tamarind and Coconut

Serves 4

- 1 cup canned **full-fat coconut milk,** well stirred
- 1 tablespoon plus 1 teaspoon **tamarind concentrate,** such as Tamicon brand
- 2 teaspoons **light brown sugar**
- 1¾ teaspoons **kosher salt**
- ⅛ teaspoon freshly ground **black pepper**
- 1½ cups **Carolina long-grain rice**
- ⅓ cup sliced **scallions,** plus more for garnish
- 3 tablespoons **neutral oil,** such as avocado or canola
- 2 tablespoons coarsely chopped fresh **cilantro leaves**

1. In a medium saucepan, combine the coconut milk, 1 cup water, tamarind concentrate, brown sugar, salt, and pepper and bring to a boil over high heat. Stir in the rice and bring back to a boil. Reduce the heat to medium-low, cover, and cook until the liquid has been absorbed and the rice is tender, about 18 minutes.

2. Remove the pan from the heat and let sit, covered, for 5 minutes. Remove the lid and fluff the rice with a fork. Spread the rice in an even layer over a large baking sheet and let cool completely, about 30 minutes. The rice can be made up to 24 hours in advance; store it on the baking sheet, covered with plastic wrap, in the refrigerator.

3. Remove the rice from the refrigerator and use your fingers to crumble it into a large bowl. Add the scallions and use your hands to toss until combined.

4. In a large cast-iron or nonstick skillet, heat the neutral oil over medium-high heat until it begins to shimmer. Add the rice and use a heavy-duty metal spatula to immediately press the rice down into the pan until the top is flat. Cook without stirring until the bottom becomes golden brown and crispy, 4 to 5 minutes (start checking at 3 minutes to make sure you don't burn it). As the rice cooks, occasionally move the pan around the burner to make sure all areas get evenly heated. Using the spatula, flip the rice over and press down firmly on the top again. Cook until the bottom is golden brown and crispy, 3 to 5 minutes longer.

5. Transfer to a platter, garnish with the cilantro and additional scallions, and serve immediately.

Crispy Rice
with Tamarind
and Coconut

Crispy Rice
with Spinach
and Lemon

Crispy Rice
with Spinach and Lemon

1. In a large cast-iron or nonstick skillet, heat the olive oil over medium heat. Add the garlic and cook, stirring constantly, until soft, about 1 minute. Add the spinach and cook until just wilted, 2 to 3 minutes. Season with salt and pepper. Transfer to a fine-mesh sieve set over a medium bowl and use the back of a spatula or spoon to press down on the spinach to remove any excess liquid. Cool completely, then roughly chop the spinach. Refrigerate until ready to use.

2. In a medium saucepan, combine 2 cups water, 1½ teaspoons kosher salt, and ⅛ teaspoon pepper and bring to a boil over high heat. Stir in the rice and bring back to a boil. Reduce the heat to medium-low, cover, and cook until the liquid has been absorbed and the rice is tender, about 18 minutes.

3. Follow step 2 on page 79.

4. Remove the rice from the refrigerator and use your fingers to crumble it into a large bowl. Add the chopped spinach, cumin, coriander, and half of the lemon zest and use your hands to toss until combined.

5. Follow step 4 on page 79, using the 3 tablespoons neutral oil.

6. Transfer to a platter, garnish with the remaining lemon zest, and serve immediately.

Serves 4

1 tablespoon extra-virgin olive oil

2 garlic cloves, finely chopped to a paste with ¼ teaspoon kosher salt

4 cups lightly packed baby spinach (about 5 ounces)

Kosher salt and freshly ground black pepper

1½ cups Carolina long-grain rice

¼ teaspoon ground cumin

¼ teaspoon ground coriander

Finely grated zest of 1 lemon

3 tablespoons neutral oil, such as avocado or canola

Napa Cabbage Fried Rice

You know that quarter of a cabbage head in the bottom of your refrigerator that's left over from making yet another coleslaw? Well, here's your way out! Fried rice when seasoned well is crazy satisfying. It's important to use rice that's at least a day old so that it has time to dry out a bit before frying.

1. Crack the eggs into a large bowl and whisk until light and frothy and uniform in color.

2. In a large cast-iron or nonstick skillet, heat 1 tablespoon of the neutral oil over medium heat until it just starts to shimmer. Add the eggs and gently mix using a silicone spatula or a wooden spoon until soft curds form, 1 to 2 minutes.

3. Remove from the heat (the eggs will still be somewhat wet), season with salt and pepper, and let the heat of the pan finish cooking them for another 30 seconds to 1 minute. Transfer to a bowl and set aside.

4. Wipe out the pan and heat the remaining 2 tablespoons oil over medium-high heat. Add the shallots and cook until lightly browned and tender, 3 to 4 minutes. Add the garlic, ginger, and scallion whites and cook for 1 minute. Add the cabbage and cook, stirring often, until crisp-tender and browned in spots, 3 to 4 minutes. Stir in the carrot and cook for 1 minute. Increase the heat to high and add the rice, soy sauce, and sesame oil and cook, stirring often, until the rice is hot and crispy in spots, 3 to 4 minutes. Add the reserved eggs and the scallion greens, stir, and cook until the eggs are heated through, about 1 minute. Season with salt and pepper.

5. Transfer the fried rice to a large serving bowl and garnish with chives, cilantro, and toasted sesame seeds. Serve immediately.

Serves 4

3 large eggs

3 tablespoons neutral oil, such as avocado or canola

Kosher salt and freshly ground black pepper

2 large shallots, finely diced

3 garlic cloves, finely chopped to a paste with ¼ teaspoon kosher salt

1-inch piece fresh ginger, peeled and finely minced

2 scallions, thinly sliced, white and green parts kept separate

¼ small head napa cabbage, thinly sliced (about 2 cups)

1 small carrot, julienned

3 cups cooked long-grain rice, cold (at least 1 day old)

3 tablespoons soy sauce

2 teaspoons toasted sesame oil

Sliced fresh chives, for garnish

Chopped fresh cilantro leaves, for garnish

Toasted sesame seeds, for garnish

Cast-Iron Paella

with Wild Mushrooms, Kale,
Italian Sausages, and Eggs

Serves 4

6 cups chicken stock, homemade (page 243) or store-bought

6 tablespoons extra-virgin olive oil

3 hot Italian sausages, sliced crosswise into coins ½ inch thick

6 ounces cremini mushrooms, sliced (about 4 cups)

6 ounces shiitake mushrooms, sliced (about 4 cups)

Kosher salt and freshly ground black pepper

1 small Spanish onion, finely diced

4 garlic cloves, finely chopped to a paste with ½ teaspoon kosher salt

1½ cups short-grain Spanish rice

1 cup dry white wine

1 teaspoon chopped fresh thyme leaves

4 large eggs

1 small bunch lacinato kale, ribs and stems removed, leaves coarsely chopped

Hot sauce, for drizzling

This is a direct descendant of my vegetarian version of paella with kale and wild mushrooms, which was a signature dish from my restaurant Gato. At home I tend to go the meaty route and add spicy, red pepper–flecked pork sausages to the game. But of course, you can keep things vegetarian by omitting the sausages and subbing vegetable stock for the chicken. Either way, the eggs nestled into the vegetables really fortify the dish.

1. Set an oven rack in the lowest position and preheat the oven to 425°F.

2. In a medium saucepan, bring the chicken stock to a boil over medium-high heat. Reduce the heat to low and keep at a simmer.

3. In a 12-inch cast-iron skillet, heat 2 tablespoons of the olive oil over medium-high heat. Add the sausages in an even layer and cook until browned on both sides and just cooked through, about 2 minutes. Use a slotted spoon to transfer the sausages to a baking sheet.

4. Add the mushrooms to the pan and sauté, tossing occasionally, until they release their liquid and are browned, 8 to 10 minutes. Season with salt and pepper, then transfer the mushrooms to the baking sheet with the sausages (but keep separate).

5. Add 2 tablespoons of the oil and the onion to the skillet and cook until softened, 4 to 6 minutes. Add half of the garlic and cook, stirring constantly, until soft, about 1 minute. Season with salt and pepper.

6. Add the rice, season with salt and pepper, and cook, stirring constantly, until the rice is translucent, about 3 minutes. Add the wine and cook, stirring, until completely evaporated, about 2 minutes. Return the mushrooms to the pan, stir in the thyme, and add enough stock to just cover the rice. Cook, without stirring, adding more stock as needed to keep the rice moist while cooking, until the rice is al dente and all the liquid in the skillet is absorbed, 15 to 20 minutes. You might not use all the stock, but it is important that the stock you *do* use be completely absorbed into the rice. Shake the pan after each addition of stock and occasionally move the pan around the burner to make sure the rice cooks evenly.

7. Continue to cook the rice, until a crust (socarrat) forms around the sides and bottom of the pan (the rice will smell toasted and make a light crackling sound), 6 to 8 minutes.

8. Make four shallow divots on the surface of the paella and crack an egg into each divot. Season the eggs with salt and pepper. Scatter the sausage pieces around the eggs. Transfer the pan to the oven and bake until the egg whites are just set but the yolks are still soft and runny, 7 to 10 minutes.

9. Meanwhile, in a large sauté pan, heat the remaining 2 tablespoons oil over medium-high heat. Add the remaining garlic and cook, stirring constantly, until soft, about 30 seconds. Add the kale, season with salt and pepper, and cook, tossing, until slightly wilted, about 1 minute. Add ¼ cup water to the pan and cook, tossing, until the kale is completely wilted, about 5 minutes longer.

10. Arrange the kale around the eggs and drizzle with hot sauce. Serve the paella in the pan.

Pro-Level Paella

Bobby

I love classic paella, and I know Sophie does, too. My recipe on page 84 veers pretty dramatically away from the traditional versions with shellfish, chorizo, and chicken that grace Spanish tables. But many of the same rules apply to making my paella as for the authentic Spanish version.

Don't be afraid of high heat. In Spain, the traditional way to make paella is to cook it over a live fire. The high heat of the flame is what cooks the bottom layer of the rice and makes it into a crispy crust, called the socarrat.

Resist the urge to stir the rice as it cooks. You want to leave the grains of rice in contact with the paella pan, so they really stick to it and fry up to get the nice and crispy socarrat.

Rotate the pan as you cook. If you're cooking this on your stovetop, then only a portion of the pan will fit directly over the burner. Rotating the pan ensures that more of it will get in direct contact with the heat source.

Take it outside. If you're lucky enough to have a grill, that's a great place to cook paella, since the fire gets hotter than your stovetop, and you have a larger surface area in contact with the bottom of the pan.

Sophie

The paella with mushrooms and kale on page 84 takes me back to my dad's restaurant Gato. I can still smell the paella and picture the guys coming out with a sizzling pan to mix the rice up for you at the table. It was the best dish on the menu, in my opinion. And apparently it was the most-sold dish, too, which is surprising because it was vegetarian. All I can say is it was a must-order for me and my friends when we'd visit the restaurant. When he cooks this paella at home, my dad has started adding sausages, which is okay by me because I *love* Italian sausages.

Shrimp and Tomato Risotto

A lot of home cooks tell me they are afraid to make risotto. I'm here to tell you it's actually quite easy. Sauté some aromatics, toast the rice a little in the pan, and add hot broth in intervals, allowing the grains to drink the liquid until they're soft. In this case we add the fruity and acidic flavor of tomato and one of Sophie's favorite ingredients, shrimp, to the rice party.

1. In a medium saucepan, bring the stock to a boil over medium-high. Reduce the heat to low and keep at a simmer.

2. In a large deep sauté pan, heat 2 tablespoons of the olive oil over medium-high heat until it shimmers. Season the shrimp on both sides with salt and pepper. Add the shrimp in an even layer and sear until just opaque and golden on both sides, but not cooked through, 2 to 3 minutes. Transfer the shrimp to a plate.

3. Reduce the heat to medium and add the remaining 2 tablespoons oil and the onion to the pan. Use a wooden spoon or spatula to scrape up any browned bits at the bottom of the pan and cook until the onion is softened (but not browned at all), about 5 minutes. Add the garlic and cook, stirring constantly, until soft, about 1 minute.

4. Increase the heat to high and add the wine. Cook until the wine is reduced to almost dry (there should be only a thin layer at the bottom of the pan), about 5 minutes. Reduce the heat to medium, add the rice, and season with salt and pepper. Stir until the rice is coated in the oil and wine and cook until lightly toasted, about 2 minutes.

5. Add 1 cup of the stock and cook, stirring, until absorbed, 2 to 3 minutes. Repeat with a second cup. As the rice becomes dry, add stock in ½-cup increments, cooking and stirring until the rice is just tender, 20 to 25 minutes of total cooking time. Adjust the heat as needed during the cooking process to maintain an active simmer. Stir in the tomato sauce until combined.

6. Stir in the butter until creamy and absorbed into the rice. Add the shrimp and any juices that collected on the plate back to the pan. Cook until the shrimp are opaque throughout, about 1 minute. Season to taste with salt and pepper and stir in the parsley.

7. To serve, spoon the risotto into four large serving bowls. Drizzle with more oil, garnish with chopped parsley, and serve immediately.

Serves 4

6 cups **Shrimp Stock** (page 243; see Note)

4 tablespoons **extra-virgin olive oil,** plus more for drizzling

12 extra-large **shrimp** (16/20 count), peeled and deveined (shells reserved for stock), tail off

Kosher salt and freshly ground **black pepper**

½ medium **Spanish onion,** finely diced

3 **garlic cloves,** finely chopped to a paste with ¼ teaspoon **kosher salt**

1 cup **dry white wine**

2 cups **Arborio rice**

¾ cup **Basic Tomato Sauce** (page 243)

3 tablespoons **unsalted butter**

2 tablespoons coarsely chopped fresh **flat-leaf parsley leaves,** plus more for garnish

Note: If you don't have enough shrimp shells to make the full 6 cups of shrimp stock needed here, you can substitute either water or vegetable stock for up to 3 cups.

Creamy Polenta
with Cremini Mushrooms and Taleggio

You could eat this as a hearty appetizer or vegetarian entrée, but I really like it as a side, served alongside some meat! (Think braised short ribs, grilled pork chops, or roasted chicken.) I'm not necessarily a truffle oil fan, but in this case a touch of it enhances the savory mushroom flavor even more. Go easy with the oil—just a drop or two. It's very strong and has the potential to bulldoze all the other ingredients in the dish.

1. In a medium saucepan, heat 2 tablespoons of the olive oil over medium-high heat. Add the onion and cook until softened, 3 to 5 minutes. Add the garlic and cook, stirring constantly, until soft, about 1 minute. Add the chicken stock, bring to a boil, then reduce the heat to medium-low to achieve a steady simmer and cook for 5 minutes.

2. Gradually whisk the polenta into the simmering liquid, pouring it in a steady stream. Whisk constantly until the mixture is smooth and begins to thicken, about 5 minutes. Reduce the heat to low and very gently simmer, stirring often, until tender and thickened but still creamy, 30 to 45 minutes. During the cooking process, if the mixture gets too thick but the polenta grains are not yet tender, stir in water ¼ cup at a time. The fully cooked polenta should be loose and pourable.

3. Meanwhile, in a large sauté pan, heat the remaining 2 tablespoons oil over medium-high heat. Add the mushrooms and cook, stirring occasionally, until browned and tender, about 15 minutes. Season with salt and pepper.

4. When the polenta is tender and thickened, remove the saucepan from the heat. Fold in the Taleggio, crème fraîche, Romano, and oregano. Stir until smooth. Season with salt and pepper.

5. Transfer the polenta to a large serving bowl and top with the mushrooms. Top with the truffle oil (if using), garnish with more Romano and serve immediately.

Serves 4

4 tablespoons extra-virgin olive oil

1 small Spanish onion, finely diced

2 garlic cloves, finely chopped to a paste with ¼ teaspoon kosher salt

4 cups chicken stock, homemade (page 243) or store-bought

1 cup polenta or stone-ground yellow cornmeal

12 ounces cremini mushrooms, thinly sliced (about 6 cups)

Kosher salt and freshly ground black pepper

6 ounces Taleggio cheese, rind removed and cut into pieces

¼ cup crème fraîche

⅓ cup freshly grated Pecorino Romano cheese, plus more for garnish

2 teaspoons finely chopped fresh oregano leaves

1 or 2 drops (about ⅛ teaspoon) white or black truffle oil (optional)

Grilled Polenta
with Balsamic Grilled Onions

Serves 4

Olive oil, for the baking dish

3 cups chicken stock, homemade (page 243) or store-bought

¾ cup polenta or stone-ground yellow cornmeal

¼ cup crème fraîche

½ cup freshly grated Pecorino Romano cheese

Kosher salt and freshly ground black pepper

4 tablespoons extra-virgin olive oil

2 small red onions, cut into ½-inch-thick rounds

3 tablespoons balsamic vinegar, plus more for garnish

1 tablespoon chopped fresh oregano leaves, plus whole leaves for garnish

In terms of texture, there are two kinds of polenta, creamy and firm. Really, the firm version is just a way to use up leftovers. Just spread the creamy polenta in a baking dish, throw it in the refrigerator to chill overnight, and the next day, cut it into pieces. Put it on a hot grill till it's a little crusty and garnish with some nice grilled onions and fresh herbs . . . new dish!

1. Generously grease an 8-inch square baking dish with olive oil and set aside.

2. In a small saucepan, bring the chicken stock to a boil, then reduce to a simmer. Gradually whisk the polenta into the simmering stock, pouring in a steady stream. Whisk constantly until the mixture is smooth and begins to thicken, about 5 minutes. Reduce the heat to low and very gently simmer, stirring often, until tender and thickened but still creamy, 30 to 45 minutes. During the cooking process, if the mixture gets too thick but the polenta grains are not yet tender, stir in water ¼ cup at a time. The fully cooked polenta should be loose and pourable.

3. When the polenta is tender and thickened, remove the saucepan from the heat and fold in the crème fraîche and Romano. Stir until smooth. Season with salt and pepper. Pour the polenta into the prepared baking dish. Allow to cool slightly at room temperature, then cover and refrigerate for at least 4 hours or up to overnight.

4. Preheat a charcoal or gas grill to medium-high heat. Remove the chilled polenta from the baking dish and cut into 9 equal squares (about 2½ inches). Brush with 2 tablespoons of the extra-virgin olive oil and season with salt and pepper. Grill on both sides until golden brown and crisp in spots, 2 to 3 minutes per side. Transfer to a platter.

5. Brush the sliced red onion rounds with the remaining 2 tablespoons extra-virgin olive oil and season with salt and pepper. Grill on both sides until charred in spots and tender, 3 to 4 minutes per side. In a small bowl, combine the vinegar and chopped oregano. Brush on the grilled onion rounds and grill for 1 to 2 minutes longer, turning as needed so the vinegar does not burn.

6. Top the polenta with the grilled onions and garnish with oregano leaves and a light drizzle of vinegar. Serve immediately.

Chicken

Chicken, Mushroom, and Kale Enchilada Casserole

This is one of my favorite Sunday night dishes: stacked corn tortillas layered with shredded chicken, sautéed mushrooms and kale, good melting cheese, and lots of red chile sauce, slowly baked in an oven-to-table casserole. All you need are margaritas to complete the meal.

1. Preheat the oven to 375°F. Lightly grease a 13 × 9-inch baking dish with olive oil.

2. In a large sauté pan, heat 2 tablespoons of the olive oil over medium heat. Add the garlic and cook until soft, about 30 seconds. Add the kale, season with salt and pepper, and cook, tossing occasionally, until the kale is tender, 6 to 8 minutes. Transfer to a bowl and set aside.

3. Add the remaining 3 tablespoons oil to the pan and increase the heat to medium-high. Once the oil starts to shimmer, add the mushrooms and cook until browned, stirring occasionally, about 15 minutes. Add the cilantro, season with salt and pepper, and add to the bowl with the kale.

4. Spread ¾ cup of the chile sauce over the bottom of the prepared baking dish. Cut 3 of the corn tortillas into quarters and set aside. Working with 1 whole tortilla at a time, dip it in the remaining chile sauce, then layer 3 of the tortillas into the dish. Coat 4 of the quartered tortilla pieces and use them to fill in any spots.

5. Layer with 2 cups of the chicken, half of the mushroom/kale mixture, 2 cups of the Monterey Jack, and ⅓ cup of the Cotija. Season each layer with salt and pepper.

6. Dip 3 additional whole tortillas and 4 of the quartered tortilla pieces in the chile sauce and add on top. Layer with the remaining chicken, remaining mushroom/kale mixture, 2 cups of the Monterey Jack, and ⅓ cup of the Cotija.

7. Dip the remaining 3 whole tortillas and 4 quartered tortilla pieces into the sauce and add to the casserole, spreading any remaining red chile sauce on top. Sprinkle with the remaining Monterey Jack and Cotija. Cover with foil.

8. Bake for 20 minutes, remove the foil, and continue to bake until the sauce is bubbling and the cheese is golden brown and melted, 15 to 20 minutes longer. Garnish with chopped cilantro and serve with sour cream and lime wedges.

Serves 8 to 10

Olive oil, for the baking dish

5 tablespoons extra-virgin olive oil

3 garlic cloves, finely chopped to a paste with ¼ teaspoon kosher salt

2 bunches lacinato kale, ribs and stems removed, leaves coarsely chopped (about 8 cups, lightly packed)

Kosher salt and freshly ground black pepper

1 pound cremini mushrooms, sliced (about 8 cups)

½ cup chopped fresh cilantro leaves, plus more for garnish

3 cups Tomato–Red Chile Sauce (page 244), warmed

12 (6-inch) corn tortillas

4 cups shredded cooked chicken

5 cups grated Monterey Jack cheese (about 1 pound)

1 cup crumbled Cotija cheese (about 4½ ounces)

Sour cream, for serving

Lime wedges, for serving

Green Chile Chicken Soup
with Avocado and Tortilla Chips

Serves 4 to 6

1 pound **Hatch green chiles** or **poblanos**

12 ounces **tomatillos** (3 or 4), husked, rinsed, and halved

1 **jalapeño,** stemmed and halved lengthwise

½ small **red onion,** cut into large chunks

3 **garlic cloves,** peeled

2 tablespoons **neutral oil,** such as avocado or canola

Kosher salt and freshly ground **black pepper**

¼ cup coarsely chopped fresh **cilantro leaves,** plus more for garnish

6 cups **chicken stock,** homemade (page 243) or store-bought

½ teaspoon **ground cumin**

4 cups shredded cooked **chicken**

Crushed tortilla chips, for serving

Diced **avocado,** for serving

Having homemade chicken broth around is invaluable. Sure, you can make this soup with store-bought stock—but starting from a foundation of homemade stock will make this and other southwestern-flavored soups so much better. In this case, roasted green chiles bring smokiness and that green pepper heat that makes this dish taste like New Mexico in a bowl. Sometimes I make a red version with ancho chiles and chipotles. But here I stuck with the classic and picked the green lane. A dark beer is the perfect "condiment" for either.

1. Set an oven rack in the lowest position and preheat the oven to 425°F.

2. Arrange the Hatch green chiles, tomatillos, jalapeño, red onion, and garlic cloves on a large sheet pan, keeping the vegetables separate—you'll be removing them in stages. Drizzle with the oil and season with salt and pepper. Rub the oil, salt, and pepper into the vegetables.

3. Roast in the oven, turning occasionally, until the garlic, jalapeño, and tomatillos are tender and charred on both sides, about 15 minutes. Remove them from the pan and transfer to a blender. Return the pan to the oven and roast until the Hatch green chiles and onion are tender and charred, about 10 minutes longer.

4. Add the onion to the blender. Transfer the Hatch green chiles to a bowl, cover the top with plastic, and let steam for 15 minutes. Remove the skin and seeds, then add to the blender. Add the cilantro and 1 cup of the chicken stock and season with salt and pepper. Blend to a smooth puree.

5. Pour the remaining 5 cups stock into a large saucepan, add the cumin, and bring to a simmer over medium-high heat. Stir in the chile puree and chicken. Season with salt and pepper and simmer for 15 minutes to allow the flavors to meld.

6. Ladle the soup into serving bowls and top with crushed tortilla chips, diced avocado, and chopped cilantro.

Smoky Split Chicken
with *"Automatic Brine"*

The aroma of chicken cooking outdoors is one of my favorites. I may have to create a cologne out of it at some point. It's the smell of slowly cooking crispy skin combined with the smokiness of the wood-burning grill that gets your neighbors to come by to say "hi." I use the term "automatic brine" or "automatic marinade" to signify that there's no waiting time before you cook. Just hit the chicken with brine and get started.

1. Soak the wood chips in cold water for 1 to 2 hours. Remove the chicken from the refrigerator 30 minutes before grilling, to take the chill off.

2. Make the automatic brine: In a small bowl, combine the vinegar, honey, celery seeds, cayenne, paprika, salt, and black pepper.

3. To finish: Use the tip of a sharp knife to poke holes throughout the chicken. Brush the chicken halves all over with the neutral oil and season with salt and pepper. In a heavy medium disposable pan, combine 1 cup water, the apple juice, and garlic.

4. Prepare a kettle grill with charcoal off to one side for indirect grilling and add the soaked wood chips over the coals. Put the disposable pan of steaming liquid on the bottom grate of the grill on the opposite side of the coals. Put the top grate on and close the lid of the grill to heat well. Put the chicken halves skin side down on the grill, directly over the hot coals, and cook, covered, until golden brown and the skin is lightly crispy, 8 to 12 minutes. Flip and cook on the second side until lightly browned, 4 to 6 minutes.

5. Move the chicken to the cooler side of the grill, over the pan of liquid. Liberally brush with some of the automatic brine. Put the lid of the grill on and open the vents on top halfway. Cook until the chicken reaches an internal temperature of 160°F, 1 hour to 1 hour 30 minutes, turning the chicken and brushing it with the brine every 15 minutes. Add additional briquettes as needed to keep the internal temperature of the grill between 225° and 250°F and add additional water to the pan of steaming liquid if it is running low.

Recipe continues

Serves 4

3 cups **apple wood** or **cherry wood chips**

2 (1½-pound) bone-in, skin-on **chicken halves**

Automatic Brine

½ cup **apple cider vinegar**

¼ cup **honey**

½ teaspoon **celery seeds**

¾ teaspoon **cayenne pepper**

2 teaspoons **smoked paprika**

2 teaspoons **kosher salt**

½ teaspoon freshly ground **black pepper**

To Finish

1 tablespoon **neutral oil,** such as avocado or canola

Kosher salt and freshly ground **black pepper**

2 cups **apple juice**

4 **garlic cloves,** lightly smashed

Pantry Barbecue Sauce (page 248), for serving

6. Once the chicken is fully cooked, brush it one last time with the brine, then flip it so that it is skin side down and move it directly over the coals to cook until the skin is charred in spots, about 5 minutes.

7. Transfer the chicken halves to a platter and allow them to rest for 10 minutes before serving with the barbecue sauce.

Variation: Cooking on a Gas Grill

Put the soaked wood chips into a smoke box or onto a large piece of heavy-duty foil. Fold the foil over the wood chips and seal the edges of the foil to make a packet. Use the tip of a knife or kitchen shears to poke several vents in the top. Lift up the grates on the right side of the grill and place the packet directly on the heat source of the grill, then return the grates.

Close the lid and turn the heat for the right side of the grill to medium-high until you start to see smoke coming out of the grill, about 20 minutes. Cook the chicken as directed in steps 4 and 5, adjusting the heat as needed to maintain an internal grill temperature between 225° and 250°F and adding additional water to the steaming liquid if it is running low.

Once the chicken is fully cooked, transfer it to a baking sheet and turn the left side of the grill to medium-high. Once the left side of the grill is hot, brush the chicken a last time with the brine and flip it so that it is skin side down and grill until the skin is charred in spots, about 5 minutes.

Chicken Milanese, Two Ways

I love fried chicken, so I am always trying to find different ways to sneak it into my weekly rotation. Crispy chicken Milanese is traditionally served with tomato, arugula, and Parmigiano, but I take a little creative license because, well, why not? It all works! During the warmer months, go for the version with prosciutto and Taleggio. When there's a chill in the air, go sautéed mushrooms all the way.

Chicken Milanese

Topped with Cremini Mushrooms, Burrata, and Balsamic

Serves 4

1 cup **balsamic vinegar**

1½ teaspoons **honey**

Kosher salt and freshly ground **black pepper**

2 tablespoons **extra-virgin olive oil**

12 ounces **cremini mushrooms,** thinly sliced (about 6 cups)

4 (6-ounce) boneless, skinless **chicken breasts**

½ cup **all-purpose flour**

2 large **eggs,** beaten

2 cups **panko bread crumbs**

Neutral oil, such as avocado or canola, for shallow-frying

6 ounces **burrata cheese**

1 cup packed **baby arugula** (about 1 ounce)

Hand-torn fresh **basil leaves,** for garnish

1. In a small nonreactive saucepan, cook the balsamic vinegar over medium-high heat until reduced to ⅓ cup, 6 to 8 minutes. Stir in the honey and season with salt and pepper. Transfer to a small bowl and let cool to room temperature (it will thicken as it cools).

2. In a large sauté pan, heat the olive oil over medium-high heat until it begins to shimmer. Add the mushrooms and cook until browned and tender, about 15 minutes. Season with salt and pepper. Set aside to cool to room temperature.

3. Pound, bread, and cook the chicken cutlets: Follow steps 1 through 3 on page 105.

4. Place each cutlet on a plate and top with the sautéed mushrooms and burrata cheese, lightly breaking apart the cheese with your fingers. Drizzle with some of the balsamic reduction, top with the baby arugula, and season with salt and pepper. Garnish with fresh torn basil and serve immediately.

Chicken
Milanese
Topped with
Prosciutto,
Taleggio,
Arugula,
and Red Wine
Vinaigrette

Chicken
Milanese
Topped with
Cremini
Mushrooms,
Burrata,
and Balsamic

Chicken Milanese

Topped with Prosciutto, Taleggio, Arugula, and Red Wine Vinaigrette

Serves 4

4 (6-ounce) boneless, skinless chicken breasts

½ cup all-purpose flour

2 large eggs, beaten

2 cups panko bread crumbs

Kosher salt and freshly ground black pepper

Neutral oil, such as avocado or canola, for shallow-frying

4 ounces Taleggio cheese, thinly sliced, at room temperature

1½ teaspoons Dijon mustard

2 tablespoons red wine vinegar

½ teaspoon honey

2 tablespoons extra-virgin olive oil

1 cup packed baby arugula (about 1 ounce)

8 thin slices prosciutto

1. Place a chicken breast between two sheets of wax or parchment paper. Pound with a meat mallet, rolling pin, or heavy skillet until ¼ inch thick. The thinner and more even, the better. Repeat with the remaining chicken.

2. Place the flour, eggs, and bread crumbs in three separate shallow baking dishes. Season each with salt and pepper. Set a wire rack in a sheet pan. Season the chicken on both sides with salt and pepper. Dredge each breast in the flour and shake off the excess. Next, dip into the egg and let any excess drip off. Finally, dredge in the bread crumbs, pressing to help the crumbs adhere evenly on both sides. Transfer the breaded chicken to the wire rack. This step can be done up to 30 minutes in advance.

3. Set another wire rack over a sheet pan and have at the ready. In a large deep sauté pan, heat ½ inch of neutral oil over medium heat until the oil begins to shimmer. Working in batches so as not to crowd the pan, cook the cutlets in a single layer until golden brown on each side and cooked through, about 3 minutes per side. Transfer the cutlets to the wire rack.

4. Immediately top the chicken with the sliced Taleggio cheese. Let the cutlets rest a few minutes while you make the salad.

5. In a small bowl, combine the mustard, vinegar, and honey and season with salt and pepper. Stream in the olive oil slowly and whisk quickly to emulsify. Put the arugula in a medium bowl and season it with salt and pepper. Drizzle 1 tablespoon of dressing around the sides of the bowl, then use tongs to lightly dress the arugula.

6. Set each cutlet on a plate and drape the prosciutto over the top. Drizzle some of the dressing over the chicken, then top with the salad and serve immediately.

Milanese 101

Sophie

Chicken Milanese feels like home to me. Whenever I'm at my dad's house, I can always count on him to cook two things: some sort of pasta and some sort of chicken cutlet. Always. I think it stems from Dad's love for chicken parmesan; chicken parm is his ultimate comfort food. But now he's branched out in all these creative ways. Recently he started topping the cutlets with delicious sautéed mushrooms and arugula. It really opened my eyes to all the many ways you can top a chicken cutlet, beyond the Italian American classic of red sauce and mozzarella.

Bobby

I could devote an entire chapter to my and Sophie's obsession with fried chicken. It's one of the greatest foods on the planet. Although fried chicken has a reputation for being a humble dish, it's actually pretty hard to get right. Two things have to happen: You want it crispy and golden brown on the outside, but also perfectly cooked on the inside. Getting both the internal temperature and external texture right isn't easy (and there's nothing worse than a bird that's somehow both raw and burned at the same time).

That's why I like to encourage Sophie and other beginner cooks to try chicken cutlets, which are chicken pieces that are sliced and/or pounded to a uniform thickness, then breaded and fried. So many cultures have their version of a breaded cutlet, which is what we call it here in the US. But in Austria and Germany, it's Wiener schnitzel; in Italy, it's milanese; in Japan, it's katsu. Because the meat is boneless and pounded thin, it cooks quickly on the inside. If you get your frying oil to the right temperature, the meat should finish cooking at the exact moment the crust is golden brown.

Pound the meat to an even thickness. If you have a particularly large piece of meat (say, a really thick chicken breast), your best bet might be to cut it crosswise into two thinner pieces, then pound those pieces to an even thickness.

Get the oil to the right temp. If it's too hot, the cutlets will brown too quickly and the crust will finish before the meat. Too cold, and the crust will be greasy.

Have fun with the toppings. My personal Milanese approach is to treat the cutlet as a giant, crispy canvas for a seasonal salad. It's the best of both worlds: panfried, crispy protein with a handful of fresh and flavorful salad on top!

Fried Chicken Thighs
with Homemade Ranch Dressing

Serves 4

4 cups buttermilk, well shaken

Kosher salt

1 tablespoon hot sauce, such as Tabasco

8 (5- to 6-ounce) bone-in, skin-on chicken thighs

2 cups all-purpose flour

½ cup cornstarch

1 teaspoon chile de árbol powder or cayenne pepper

1½ teaspoons garlic powder

1½ teaspoons onion powder

1½ teaspoons sweet paprika

Freshly ground black pepper

Neutral oil, such as avocado or canola, for deep-frying

Ranch Dressing (page 248), for serving

Sophie and I share a love for chicken thighs. It's the best part of the bird! So when I don't feel like butchering a whole chicken (even professional cooks have those moments), I just buy straight thighs. It took me a little while to come around to ranch, but now I'm fully converted. It's one of America's favorite flavors and it's easy to see why. Bring the tang to your chicken!

1. In a large bowl or large baking dish, combine 2 cups of the buttermilk, 1 tablespoon salt, and the hot sauce. Add the chicken thighs and turn to coat. Cover and refrigerate for at least 4 hours and up to overnight. Drain the chicken thighs in a colander, transfer to a baking sheet, and pat them very dry.

2. Set up a dredging station: Place the remaining 2 cups buttermilk in a medium bowl. In a large bowl, combine the flour, cornstarch, chile de árbol powder, garlic powder, onion powder, and paprika. Season with salt and pepper and whisk to combine. Divide the mixture between two shallow bowls. For an extra-craggy, crispy crust, drizzle a couple of spoonfuls of buttermilk into the second bowl of seasoned flour, and use your fingers to create some flour clumps.

3. Set a wire rack in a sheet pan. Working in batches of 3 or 4, dredge the thighs in the first bowl of seasoned flour and shake off the excess, then dip in the buttermilk and allow the excess to drain off. Dredge in the second bowl of seasoned flour and shake off the excess. Put the chicken pieces on the wire rack to sit while the oil heats.

4. Pour about 2 inches of neutral oil into a deep cast-iron skillet or large Dutch oven; the oil should not come more than halfway up the sides of the pot. Put the pot over medium-high heat and heat the oil to 375°F on a deep-fry thermometer.

5. Set up a clean wire rack over a second sheet pan. Add 4 of the chicken thighs to the hot oil and fry, turning the pieces occasionally, until evenly golden brown and cooked through, about 10 minutes. While the chicken cooks, adjust the heat as needed to maintain the oil temperature between 300° and 325°F. Remove the thighs from the oil with a slotted spoon and transfer to the wire rack to drain. Bring the oil back to 375°F and repeat with the remaining chicken thighs.

6. Serve hot with the ranch dressing on the side.

Note: *Make sure to give your frying oil time to come back to temperature in between batches, so your chicken's skin gets crisp but not greasy.*

— 66 —

Fried chicken is one of our favorite foods ever. When we go to the Saratoga Race Course in upstate New York, we always end up eating fried chicken from a local restaurant called Hattie's. Like, every day. We just can't stop. —SF

— 99 —

Chicken Legs in Tomato Curry

Serves 4

This recipe calls for chicken legs because that's what I had on hand the first time I made it. But you could also make it with chicken thighs. Make sure to buy a good-quality Madras curry. Good-quality spices make good-quality meals.

1. Set an oven rack in the middle position and preheat the oven to 400°F. Place a wire rack inside of a sheet pan.

2. In a large deep sauté pan, heat the oil over medium-high heat until it shimmers. Season the chicken legs all over with salt, pepper, and 2 teaspoons of the curry powder. Add the chicken to the pan and sear until the skin is well browned and crusty, 5 to 7 minutes per side, adjusting the heat as needed so the curry powder doesn't burn.

3. Transfer the chicken legs to the wire rack on the sheet pan and bake until cooked through, 15 to 20 minutes.

4. In the same pan that you seared the chicken, add the onion and both mustard seeds and cook until the onion is golden brown in spots and tender, about 8 minutes. Add the garlic, ginger, and remaining 2 teaspoons curry powder and cook for 1 minute. Stir in the tomatoes and sugar and season with salt and pepper. Bring to a strong simmer and cook, using a potato masher to lightly crush the tomatoes as they cook, until most of the tomato juice has reduced and the sauce has thickened, 10 to 15 minutes.

5. In a small bowl, season the yogurt with salt and pepper and stir until smooth. Stir in 1 to 3 tablespoons water to thin out the yogurt so it drizzles easily off a spoon.

6. Spoon the tomato curry onto a large rimmed platter and add the roasted chicken legs. Drizzle the yogurt over the chicken, garnish with the cilantro leaves, and serve.

2 tablespoons neutral oil, such as avocado or canola

4 (8-ounce) bone-in, skin-on chicken leg quarters

Kosher salt and freshly ground black pepper

4 teaspoons hot Madras curry powder

1 large Spanish onion, finely diced

1 teaspoon yellow mustard seeds

1 teaspoon black mustard seeds

4 garlic cloves, grated (about 1 tablespoon)

1 tablespoon grated fresh ginger

1 (28-ounce) can whole peeled plum tomatoes and their juices

Pinch of sugar

½ cup 2% plain Greek yogurt

Fresh cilantro leaves, for garnish

Red Curry Roasted Chicken
with Ginger and Lemongrass

Serves 4

I have my good friend Jet Tila to thank for this recipe. I heard him talking about it somewhere and realized that I had many of the key ingredients, like red curry paste and coconut milk, in my pantry already. If you want a full-flavored version of a roasted chicken on a Sunday night, try this one. Your taste buds will be dancing for hours. Thanks, Jet!

Note: You can either butterfly the bird yourself by using poultry shears to cut along both sides of the backbone and removing it or you can ask your butcher to do it.

1. In a blender, combine the ginger, garlic, lemongrass, scallions, cilantro, honey, 1 tablespoon pepper, the curry powder, curry paste, tamari, and coconut milk. Blend until smooth.

2. Pour the marinade into a 2-gallon resealable plastic storage bag set inside a large bowl. Add the chicken to the marinade, seal the bag, and massage the marinade into the chicken. Refrigerate for at least 4 hours and up to 8 hours.

3. Remove the chicken from the refrigerator 30 minutes before cooking, to take the chill off. Set an oven rack in the middle position and preheat the oven to 375°F.

4. Line a large sheet pan with foil and set a wire rack on the foil. Lay the chicken skin side up on the rack and tuck the wings under the chicken. Roast until the chicken is cooked through and the juices run clear, 45 minutes to 1 hour.

5. Remove from the oven and rest for at least 10 minutes.

6. Preheat a charcoal or gas grill to medium-high heat and lightly oil the grates. (Or if cooking indoors, preheat your oven's broiler.) Place the chicken skin side down on the grill (or on a sheet pan with a wire rack, skin side up under the broiler) and cook until the skin is lightly charred in spots, 5 to 10 minutes. Remove from the grill (or broiler) and let rest for 5 minutes.

7. Cut the chicken into pieces, garnish with cilantro leaves, and serve with lime wedges and sweet chili sauce on the side.

1 tablespoon grated fresh ginger

6 garlic cloves, grated (about 2 tablespoons)

2 tablespoons finely minced lemongrass

2 tablespoons sliced scallions

2 tablespoons chopped fresh cilantro leaves

1 tablespoon honey

Freshly ground black pepper

2 tablespoons curry powder

¼ cup red curry paste

¼ cup tamari

1 cup canned full-fat coconut milk, well stirred

4-pound whole chicken, butterflied, backbone removed (see Note)

Neutral oil, such as avocado or canola, for the grill

Fresh cilantro leaves, for garnish

Lime wedges, for serving

Thai-style sweet chili sauce, for serving

Butterflied Spice-Rubbed Roasted Chicken

with Rosemary, Shallots, and Lemon

I have to give a shout-out to the G.O.A.T. roast chicken queen, Ina Garten. This recipe is a blatant steal of one of her recipes in *Cooking for Jeffrey*, with a few minor changes. Let's give credit where it belongs. Ina's recipes just flat-out work, and this roasted chicken has become one of Sophie's and my favorites.

1. Set an oven rack in the middle position and preheat the oven to 450°F.

2. In a spice grinder or mortar, combine the rosemary, fennel seeds, and mustard seeds and pulse or grind into a fine powder. Transfer to a small bowl and stir in 1 tablespoon salt and 2 teaspoons pepper. Add the olive oil and stir to combine. Set aside.

3. Pat the chicken dry with paper towels on all sides. On the bottom of a large cast-iron skillet or roasting pan, spread out the lemon slices, shallots, and garlic in a single layer. Season with salt and pepper. Place the chicken skin side down on top of the lemon/shallot mixture and brush with about half of the oil/herb/spice mixture. Turn the chicken over so that it is skin side up and brush it with the remaining oil/herb/spice mixture.

4. Roast the chicken for 35 minutes. Pour the wine directly onto the shallots and lemons in the pan and continue to roast until the skin is golden brown, the chicken is cooked through, and the juices run clear, 20 to 30 minutes longer.

5. Remove the chicken from the oven and allow it to rest for 10 to 15 minutes. Cut the chicken into pieces, spoon on some of the lemon/shallot mixture, garnish with the parsley, and serve.

Serves 4

2 teaspoons fresh rosemary leaves

2 teaspoons fennel seeds

1 teaspoon yellow mustard seeds

Kosher salt and freshly ground black pepper

⅓ cup extra-virgin olive oil

4-pound whole chicken, butterflied, backbone removed (see Note, page 112)

1 lemon, cut into slices ¼ inch thick

4 large shallots, cut into slices ¼ inch thick

6 garlic cloves, lightly smashed

½ cup dry rosé wine

2 tablespoons chopped fresh flat-leaf parsley leaves

Butterfly Your Bird

Sophie

One of the first things my dad wanted me to learn how to cook was roasted chicken. Now, whenever I make anything chicken-related, I pump it up with a lot of rosemary, a lot of lemons, and a lot of shallots. (One of my favorite quarantine tweets—I forget who wrote it—was, "Why didn't anyone tell me about shallots?!" So funny, and so relatable, because when I first discovered shallots I definitely had one of those "Where have you been all my life?" moments, too.)

Bobby

Knowing how to roast a chicken is one of those essential techniques that will serve you for the rest of your life. A roast chicken is never going out of style. Ask ten different people how to roast a chicken, though, and you'll get ten different answers. What most people agree on is you want a bronzed, crisped skin with moist, tender meat inside. And you want everything—skin, white meat, and dark meat—to finish cooking at the same time. *That* is the tricky part.

My favorite way to cook a chicken is to butterfly it first. Some people use the term *spatchcock*, but it means the same thing. Butterflying is a great technique because it helps the chicken cook faster and more evenly, so the breast is less likely to dry out before the legs and thighs are done.

When I showed this technique to Sophie, she laughed and said it seems like you have to be really strong to do it. You don't need to be strong, though. You just need a sharp knife or good shears. Of course, you could ask your butcher to butterfly the chicken for you, but where's the fun in that?

Remove the backbone. Turn the chicken breast side down. Using a knife or kitchen shears (I prefer a knife, but use whatever is easiest for you), cut down either side of the backbone. You might have to use a little force to disconnect the backbone where it connects with the thigh bones. If you want to be a pro, save the backbone for stock.

Smash it flat. Flip the bird over so it's breast side up and push down on it to crack the rib bones a bit and flatten the bird.

Cook breast-side up. Place the bird skin side up in your roasting pan and cook as instructed.

Chicken Soup à la Mrs. Kretchmer

Serves 6 to 8

4- to 5-pound **whole chicken**

2 **carrots,** coarsely chopped

2 **celery stalks,** coarsely chopped

1 medium **Spanish onion,** unpeeled, halved

2 **bay leaves**

6 sprigs **thyme**

12 sprigs **flat-leaf parsley leaves**

¼ teaspoon **black peppercorns**

Kosher salt and freshly ground **black pepper**

Chopped fresh **dill,** for garnish

Crushed soda crackers and/or **potato chips,** for garnish

My best friend and forever business partner, Laurence Kretchmer, fancies himself an expert pizza maker. So he's probably annoyed that the only time I ever go to him for culinary advice is when I want him to ask his mother, Dorothy, for tips on this classic chicken soup. She taught it to me more than twenty-five years ago and it's still my go-to. It's all about starting with a whole chicken and a whole Spanish onion with its skin left on. The skin imparts flavor but also a golden hue to the broth. I'm a believer that this soup has healing properties. One sniffle in my house and soup's on!

Note: If you're pressed for time, instead of covering the chicken with just water, use a mixture of water and 4 cups store-bought low-sodium chicken stock and then reduce the cooking time to 1½ hours.

1. In a stockpot, combine the chicken, carrots, celery, onion, bay leaves, thyme, parsley, peppercorns, and 2 teaspoons of salt. Add enough cold water to cover the chicken completely. Bring to a boil over high heat. Reduce the heat to low and simmer until the chicken is very tender and the meat is falling off the bone, about 3 hours.

2. Use tongs to remove the chicken from the pot and transfer to a large plate or baking sheet. When cool enough to handle, remove the skin and discard. Use your fingers to separate the chicken breast and thigh meat from the bones. Discard the bones. Use two forks to pull the meat apart into soft chunks or use a knife and cut into bite-size pieces.

3. Strain the stock into a large bowl and discard all the solids. Return the stock to the pot and bring to a boil over high heat. Cook until slightly reduced and the flavor has intensified, about 15 minutes. Return the chicken back to the stock and cook for 5 minutes. Season with salt and pepper.

4. Ladle into serving bowls and garnish with chopped dill and serve with crushed crackers and/or potato chips.

Meat

Fennel and Paprika Rubbed Pork Chops
with Peach Agrodolce

Serves 4

1 tablespoon fennel seeds

2 teaspoons smoked paprika

4 (8-ounce) boneless pork loin chops, at least ¾ inch thick

1 tablespoon neutral oil, such as avocado or canola

3 peaches

1¼ cups red wine vinegar

6 tablespoons honey

Kosher salt and freshly ground black pepper

2 teaspoons extra-virgin olive oil, plus more for drizzling

2 tablespoons hand-torn fresh basil leaves

Pork chops always remind me of my childhood. They were one of my mom's go-to moves. Dame Dorothy might not have seasoned hers with fennel and paprika, but I still like to think that her influence is being passed down through me to her only grandchild, Sophie. Hopefully Sophie will keep the tradition going and develop her own signature version.

1. Put the fennel seeds into a spice grinder or mortar and pulse or grind into a fine powder. Transfer to a small bowl, add the paprika, and stir to combine.

2. Brush the pork chops all over with the neutral oil and rub with the fennel/paprika mixture. Let sit at room temperature for 30 minutes.

3. Meanwhile, halve, pit, and chop 2 of the peaches. Add to a small saucepan along with the vinegar and honey. Bring to a boil over medium-high, then reduce the heat to medium-low and simmer until syrupy and reduced by two-thirds, 20 to 25 minutes. Strain through a fine-mesh sieve set over a bowl, pressing down slightly on the peaches to extract extra flavor (discard the solids). Season the liquid with salt and pepper and set the peach agrodolce aside to cool.

4. Preheat a charcoal or gas grill to medium-high heat. (Or if cooking indoors, preheat a grill pan or large cast-iron skillet over medium-high heat.) Season the pork chops all over with salt and pepper. Place the pork chops on the grill (or grill pan or skillet) and cook until charred on the first side, 3 to 5 minutes. Turn the pork chops over and cook until charred on the second side and the pork is just cooked through, 3 to 5 minutes.

5. Remove the pork chops from the heat and immediately brush all over with the agrodolce. Allow to rest for 5 minutes.

6. Meanwhile, cut the remaining peach in half, remove the pit, and cut into wedges ¼ inch thick. Brush with the olive oil and season with salt and pepper. Grill (or pan-sear) until charred in spots on both sides and just tender, about 1 minute per side. Transfer to a bowl and toss with the basil.

7. Serve the pork chops topped with the peach slices and drizzled with additional agrodolce and olive oil.

Korean-Style Pork Lettuce Wraps

I love the flavors of Korean food. The more I learn about traditional Korean ingredients like gochujang (a hot pepper paste) and kimchi, the more I want to keep cooking with them. This dish is satisfying on so many levels. It has tons of flavor, contrasting textures like soft, silky pork and crunchy raw veg, and it feels really healthy. Plus there's a nice communal element, since you set out all the components on the table and encourage people to make their own wraps with lettuce, rice, kimchi, pork, and sauce. Flavorful, healthy, and fun to eat? Okay, I'm in.

1. Prepare the pork: In a large bowl or baking dish, combine the garlic, ginger, honey, tamari, neutral oil, orange juice, and gochujang. Whisk until smooth. Measure ¾ cup of the marinade and refrigerate for later. Add the pork to the bowl or baking dish with the remaining marinade. Turn to coat, cover with plastic wrap, and refrigerate for at least 1 hour and up to 8 hours.

2. Remove the pork from the refrigerator 30 minutes before cooking.

3. Preheat a charcoal or gas grill to medium-high heat and lightly oil the grates.

4. While the grill heats up, add ½ cup of the reserved marinade to a small saucepan. Bring to a simmer over medium heat and cook for 2 minutes. Transfer to a small serving bowl and set the sauce aside.

5. Remove the pork from the marinade, allow any excess marinade to drip away, and season all over with salt. Grill, turning occasionally and basting with the remaining reserved ¼ cup marinade, until deeply charred in spots and cooked to medium doneness, 5 to 8 minutes. Transfer the pork to a cutting board and let rest for 5 minutes.

6. To serve: Thinly slice the pork ½ inch thick and serve on a platter alongside the sauce, butter lettuce leaves, kimchi, rice, scallions, cilantro, and sesame seeds.

Serves 4

Pork

4 garlic cloves, grated (about 1 tablespoon)

1 tablespoon grated fresh ginger

2 tablespoons honey

3 tablespoons tamari

3 tablespoons neutral oil, such as avocado or canola, plus more for the grill

½ cup orange juice

½ cup gochujang

1½ pounds boneless, skinless pork shoulder

Kosher salt

For Serving

Butter lettuce leaves

Good-quality prepared kimchi

Cooked short-grain rice

Sliced scallions

Fresh cilantro leaves

Toasted sesame seeds

—— 66 ——

Korean food is me and my dad's jam. Korean-style pork, Korean-style chicken, Korean-style anything . . . we are on that train. With kimchi, rice, and a great beer on the side, who can resist? —SF

—————— 99 —

Pan-Seared Pork Chops
with Red Chile–Pineapple Sauce

Serves 4

1 lengthwise quarter of a fresh pineapple, peeled and cored (about 10 ounces)

2 ancho chiles, stemmed and seeded

2 chiles de árbol, stemmed and seeded

½ small red onion, cut into large chunks

2 garlic cloves, peeled

1 cup canned tomato puree

1½ cups chicken stock, homemade (page 243) or store-bought, plus more as needed

½ teaspoon ground cumin

⅛ teaspoon ground allspice

⅛ teaspoon ground cinnamon

Kosher salt

1 tablespoon honey

4 (10- to 12-ounce) bone-in center-cut pork chops, at least ¾ inch thick (see Note)

1 tablespoon sliced scallions

1 teaspoon extra-virgin olive oil, plus additional for garnish

Freshly ground black pepper

4 tablespoons neutral oil, such as avocado or canola

The real star of this dish is the sauce, which is a play off the Mexican classic manchamanteles, a mole featuring pineapple and chiles. I like to serve this sauce with pork or chicken in any iteration; it just so happened that I had some thick bone-in chops that needed a little sweet and spicy kick.

Note: If your chops are thicker than 1 inch, you may want to finish them in the oven to ensure they cook evenly. Preheat the oven to 400°F. Pan-sear both sides of the pork chops as directed, then transfer to the oven and cook until the pork chops reach an internal temperature of 140°F.

1. Cut the pineapple lengthwise into ½-inch planks and set aside.

2. In a large sauté pan, toast the ancho chiles and chiles de árbol over medium-high heat until browned in spots and pliable, turning frequently, about 30 seconds for the chiles de árbol and 1 to 2 minutes for the ancho chiles. Transfer the chiles to a baking sheet to cool slightly. In the same sauté pan, cook the red onion and garlic cloves until charred in spots, turning occasionally, 2 to 3 minutes for the garlic and 5 to 7 minutes for the onion. Transfer to the baking sheet.

3. In the same sauté pan, cook the pineapple planks until deeply charred on all sides, 6 to 10 minutes. Reserve two of the planks for garnish.

4. Transfer the remaining pineapple planks to a large saucepan and add the tomato puree, chicken stock, cumin, allspice, and cinnamon. Season with salt. Stir to combine and use a wooden spoon or spatula to scrape up any charred bits in the saucepan and to break up the pineapple. Add the toasted chiles, onion, and garlic to the saucepan. Stir to combine. Bring to a boil over medium-high heat, then reduce to low and cook until the chiles are completely softened, stirring occasionally, about 20 minutes.

Recipe continues

5. Transfer the mixture to a blender and add the honey. Remove the steam vent from the center of the lid, cover the small opening with a kitchen towel (this will help to release steam), and blend until smooth. Set a fine-mesh sieve inside of the saucepan you cooked the sauce in and pour the sauce through the sieve. Use the back of a spoon to help push down on the solids (discard the solids). The consistency should be similar to a silky enchilada sauce. If needed, stir in additional stock, 1 tablespoon at a time, until that consistency is reached. Cover with a lid and keep warm on low heat while you cook the pork chops.

6. Remove the pork chops from the refrigerator 30 minutes before cooking, to take the chill off.

7. Meanwhile, cut the two reserved pineapple planks into a ½-inch dice and transfer to a small bowl. Add the scallions and olive oil and season with salt and pepper. Stir to combine and then set aside.

8. Season the pork chops on all sides with salt and pepper. In a large cast-iron skillet, heat 2 tablespoons of the neutral oil over high heat until the oil starts to shimmer. Add 2 of the pork chops and sear on the first side, 3 to 4 minutes. Flip and sear until the pork is cooked to medium doneness, 2 to 5 minutes (depending on the thickness of the pork chops). Transfer the cooked pork chops to a baking sheet. Remove the pan from the heat and carefully pour the used oil into a small heatproof bowl (once cooled, discard the oil). Add the remaining 2 tablespoons neutral oil to the skillet and cook the remaining 2 pork chops.

9. Spoon some of the red chile–pineapple sauce onto four individual serving plates. Add a cooked pork chop to each plate and top with more of the sauce. Garnish each pork chop with some of the diced pineapple and scallion mixture, then drizzle with additional olive oil and serve immediately. Cool any leftover red chile–pineapple sauce completely, then transfer to an airtight container and store in the refrigerator for up to 5 days or in the freezer for up to 3 months.

Oven-Roasted Porchetta
with Salsa Verde

This reminds me of walking down the streets of Florence with my dad and hitting a food truck that sold porchetta sandwiches slathered with salsa verde. Obviously, I've passed down my father's love for this classic Italian specialty to Sophie. Making it at home is definitely work—but for the holidays or a party, it's a showstopper and definitely worth the effort. The key is to start at high heat and turn the outer skin of the pork belly into a sort of crackling. Once the skin is crisped up, you reduce the heat for the duration of the cook. This ensures juiciness inside. I love to cook this outside over live fire, which you can do if your grill is big enough and has a rotisserie attachment.

1. Make the porchetta: In a large saucepan, bring 6 cups water to a boil over medium-high heat. Add ½ cup kosher salt and the sugar and cook until dissolved. Add 4 of the garlic cloves, the bay leaves, and black peppercorns and remove from the heat. Stir in the ice cubes until the ice is melted and the brine is completely cooled. Transfer the brine to a very large bowl or a large plastic storage container. Add the pork loin, cover, and refrigerate for at least 1 hour and up to 4 hours.

2. Meanwhile, line a large sheet pan with foil and set a wire rack on top of the foil. Set aside.

3. Heat a small sauté pan over medium heat. Spread the fennel seeds in a single layer in the pan and toast until fragrant, shaking the pan frequently, 2 to 3 minutes. Transfer to a spice grinder or mortar, cool completely, then pulse or grind to a fine powder.

4. In a food processor, combine the ground fennel, the remaining 6 garlic cloves, the rosemary, orange zest, Calabrian chile paste, mustard, olive oil, 4 teaspoons salt, and 1½ teaspoons black pepper. Blend until the mixture becomes a coarse paste. Set the seasoning paste aside.

5. Remove the pork from the brine and dry very well with paper towels. On a large cutting board, lay the pork belly skin side down with a long side facing you. Arrange the pork loin along the center of the pork belly (the pork loin should be perpendicular to you). Trim away any overhanging ends of

Recipe continues

Serves 8 to 12

Porchetta

Kosher salt

¼ cup sugar

10 garlic cloves, lightly smashed

2 bay leaves

1 tablespoon black peppercorns

4 cups ice cubes

2½ to 3 pounds boneless center-cut pork loin

3 tablespoons fennel seeds

⅓ cup coarsely chopped fresh rosemary leaves

Finely grated zest of 2 oranges

2 to 3 tablespoons Calabrian chile paste

3 tablespoons Dijon mustard

⅓ cup extra-virgin olive oil

Freshly ground black pepper

5- to 6-pound piece skin-on pork belly

Salsa Verde

¾ cup extra-virgin olive oil

2 garlic cloves, finely chopped to a paste with ¼ teaspoon kosher salt

2 oil-packed anchovy fillets, drained and finely chopped

Finely grated zest of 1 lemon

Pinch of red pepper flakes

1 cup finely chopped fresh flat-leaf parsley leaves

¼ cup finely chopped fresh tarragon leaves

2 tablespoons sliced fresh chives

Kosher salt and freshly ground black pepper

the loin. Starting from the left, roll the belly over the loin so that the two short ends of the pork belly meet. The pork loin should be fully encased in the pork belly. If there is any overlap of the pork belly, trim it so that the two ends meet perfectly. Reserve the meat trimmings for another use.

6. Unroll the pork belly and remove the pork loin. Use a sharp knife to make a 1-inch crosshatch pattern in the flesh part of the belly (about ½ inch deep). Turn the pork belly over and use the tip of the knife to poke holes throughout the skin (the more holes, the better, since this will help the rendered fat come up through the skin and make it crisp up better). Season the skin liberally with salt and black pepper.

7. Turn the pork belly over again so it is skin side down and rub the seasoning paste evenly on the flesh side of the pork belly and on the pork loin. Turn the pork belly so that a long side is facing you, lay the pork loin down the center of the belly (perpendicular to you), then starting from the left, roll the belly over the loin so that the two short ends meet.

8. Use butcher's twine to tightly tie the pork belly together so that the pork loin is securely encased in the pork belly. Transfer the porchetta seam side down to the rack in the lined sheet pan. Refrigerate, uncovered, for at least 12 hours and up to 48 hours.

9. On the day that you cook the porchetta, make the salsa verde: In a medium bowl, combine the olive oil, garlic, anchovies, lemon zest, and pepper flakes. Whisk to combine, then stir in the parsley, tarragon, and chives. Season with salt and black pepper and let the salsa verde sit at room temperature to allow the flavors to meld while you cook the porchetta.

10. Remove the porchetta from the refrigerator 2 hours before cooking. Set an oven rack in the middle position and preheat the oven to 450°F.

11. Roast the porchetta for 30 minutes. Reduce the oven temperature to 325°F and continue cooking until the skin is golden brown and an instant-read thermometer inserted into the center of the meat registers 140°F, 1½ to 2½ hours longer.

12. Remove the porchetta from the oven. Carefully transfer it to a second baking sheet. Lift the wire rack from the sheet pan the porchetta was cooked on and carefully pour any fat that collected on the foil into a small heatproof bowl (once cooled, discard the fat). Return the rack to the foil-lined pan and set the porchetta on the rack.

13. Turn the broiler to high. Broil the porchetta, rotating frequently, until the skin bubbles and becomes crispy and crackly, 8 to 15 minutes (the timing for this will depend heavily on your broiler).

14. Rest the porchetta for 30 minutes. Cut away the twine, then slice the pork with a serrated knife and serve immediately with the salsa verde.

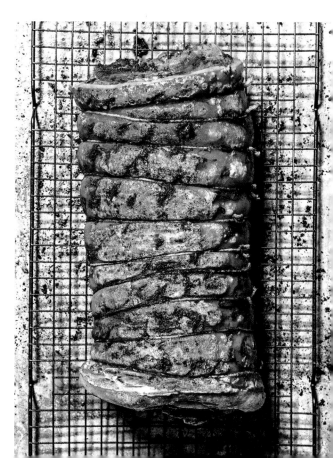

Hoisin Ribs
with Crunchy Garlic, Peanuts, and Scallions

Hoisin sauce is an ingredient that I love but frankly don't use as much as I should. It has a tart, fermented taste with a hint of sweetness, which means it's great as a barbecue sauce. Brush it on these ribs and you'll be very happy. Promise! Sophie loves ribs and these definitely got her seal of approval.

1. Make the hoisin barbecue sauce: In a large saucepan, heat the neutral oil over medium-high heat. Add the onion, season with salt and pepper, and cook until soft, 6 to 8 minutes. Add the ginger and garlic and cook for 1 minute. Stir in the Worcestershire sauce, mustard, pureed chipotle, honey, vinegar, ketchup, and hoisin sauce. Bring to a boil, then reduce the heat to low and cook, stirring occasionally, until reduced slightly, about 15 minutes.

2. Transfer the mixture to a blender, remove the steam vent from the center of the lid, and cover the small opening with a kitchen towel (this will help to release steam). Blend until smooth. Return the mixture to the saucepan, add the lime juice, and season with salt and pepper. The sauce should be thick but pourable. If it is too thick, stir in a splash of additional lime juice or water. Refrigerate the sauce until ready to use.

3. Make the ribs: Stir together the paprika, Chinese five-spice powder, ground ginger, mustard powder, granulated garlic, pepper flakes, 4 teaspoons salt, and 1 teaspoon black pepper. Rub the spice mixture into the ribs on the top side, wrap in plastic wrap, and refrigerate for at least 4 hours and up to 24 hours.

4. Soak the wood chips in cold water for 1 to 2 hours. Remove the ribs from the refrigerator 45 minutes before grilling, to take the chill off. In a large bowl, combine 4 cups water, the soy sauce, fresh ginger, and smashed garlic and divide between two heavy disposable pans.

5. Prepare a kettle grill with charcoal off to one side for indirect grilling and add the soaked apple wood chips over the coals. Put one disposable pan of steaming liquid on the bottom grate of the grill on the opposite side of the coals. Put the top grate on and heat well. Put the ribs on the grill, top side down, directly over the hot coals, and cook until golden brown and a crust has formed, about 10 minutes. Turn the ribs over and

Recipe and ingredients continue

Serves 4 to 6

Hoisin Barbecue Sauce

2 tablespoons neutral oil, such as avocado or canola

1 small Spanish onion, diced

Kosher salt and freshly ground black pepper

1 tablespoon grated fresh ginger

4 garlic cloves, grated

1 tablespoon Worcestershire sauce

2 tablespoons Dijon mustard

1 to 2 tablespoons pureed canned chipotle peppers in adobo sauce

2 tablespoons honey

¼ cup apple cider vinegar

½ cup ketchup

¾ cup hoisin sauce

1 tablespoon fresh lime juice

Ribs

1 tablespoon plus 1½ teaspoons smoked paprika

1 tablespoon Chinese five-spice powder

1 tablespoon ground ginger

1 tablespoon mustard powder

2 teaspoons granulated garlic

1 teaspoon red pepper flakes

Kosher salt and freshly ground black pepper

2 (2½- to 3-pound) racks St. Louis–style pork ribs, membranes removed

6 cups apple wood chips

2 cups soy sauce

move the ribs to the cooler side of the grill, over the liquid, and place the other disposable pan with steaming liquid next to them over the coals. Put the lid of the grill on and open the vents on top halfway. Cook until the ribs are tender and juicy, about 2 hours. Add additional briquettes as needed to keep the internal temperature of the grill between 225° and 250°F and add additional water to the steam pan if it is running low.

6. Finish the ribs by moving them back over the hot coals and turning and basting with hoisin barbecue sauce for 10 to 20 minutes. Remove the ribs from the grill and immediately brush with more of the sauce.

7. Make the crunchy garlic topping: Line a dish with paper towels. In a medium sauté pan, heat ¼ inch of neutral oil over medium heat. Add the garlic slices and gently fry, stirring occasionally, until the slices are lightly golden brown, 4 to 8 minutes. Remove the garlic with a slotted spoon to the paper towels and sprinkle with salt. Cool slightly, then coarsely chop and add to a small bowl. Add the scallions and peanuts and stir to combine.

8. To serve, cut the ribs apart and put on a platter. Scatter the crunchy garlic topping over the top and serve with any extra hoisin barbecue sauce on the side.

½ cup thinly sliced fresh ginger

6 garlic cloves, lightly smashed

Crunchy Garlic Topping

Neutral oil, such as avocado or canola, for shallow-frying

8 garlic cloves, sliced paper thin

Kosher salt

⅓ cup sliced scallions

¼ cup unsalted roasted peanuts, coarsely chopped

Variation: Using a Gas Grill

Divide the soaked apple wood chips between two large pieces of heavy-duty aluminum foil or place them in a smoke box. Fold the foil over the wood chips and seal the edges of the foil to make two packets. Use the tip of a knife or kitchen shears to poke several vents in the top. Lift up the grates on the right side of the grill and place one of the foil packets directly on the heat source of the grill, then return the grates. Put the two disposable pans of steaming liquid on top of the grates directly over the wood chips.

Close the lid and turn the heat for the right side of the grill to medium-high until you start to see smoke coming out of the grill, about 20 minutes. Reduce the heat to medium. Open the lid and put the ribs on the left side of the grill (indirect heat). Grill the ribs slowly with the cover closed for 1½ hours, adjusting the heat as needed to maintain an internal grill temperature between 225° and 250°F. After 1½ hours, replace the spent wood chips with the second foil packet of wood chips and add additional water to the steaming liquid if it is running low. Continue to grill the ribs until they are tender, 2 to 3 hours longer.

Turn the heat on the left side of the grill to medium-high and turn the ribs over and cook until a crust has formed, about 5 minutes. Turn the ribs over again and brush the top side with some of the hoisin barbecue sauce. Continue grilling and basting the ribs until they are charred in spots, 10 to 15 minutes. Remove the ribs from the grill and immediately brush with more of the sauce.

Corned Beef
with Sweet-and-Sour Cabbage and Kale

I'm always trying to do something inventive and flavorful with corned beef, especially for St. Patrick's Day, which is an important holiday in my family. I usually try to spend it with my dad, Bill Flay, better known to Sophie as Papa. Sometimes we celebrate at one of our favorite Irish pubs and other times at my kitchen table. For this recipe, I rely on the sweet and sour of the cabbage and some hot and sweet mustard I serve on the side to wake up that boiled beef a little.

1. Place the corned beef in a large pot and cover with cold water by 1 inch. Bring to a boil over high heat, then cover, reduce the heat to medium-low, and simmer until tender, 2½ to 3 hours, adding more water if needed to keep the beef submerged. Drain the beef and let cool for 30 minutes.

2. Meanwhile, make the mustard sauce: In a medium bowl, combine the Dijon mustard, whole-grain mustard, honey, and horseradish and whisk until smooth. Season with salt and pepper. Set aside at room temperature for at least 30 minutes to allow the flavors to meld.

3. Make the sweet-and-sour cabbage and kale: In a large Dutch oven, heat the olive oil over medium-high heat until it begins to shimmer. Add the onion and cook until lightly browned in spots and tender, about 5 minutes. Add the garlic and cook until soft, about 30 seconds. Add the red cabbage and green cabbage, season with salt and pepper, and cook until the cabbage is just starting to wilt, about 3 minutes. Add the kale, caraway seeds, vinegar, and honey and cook until the cabbage and kale are crisp-tender, stirring occasionally, about 5 minutes. Stir in ½ cup water and continue cooking until the vegetables are very tender and the water has evaporated, 6 to 8 minutes. Stir in the butter, season with salt and pepper, and remove from the heat. Cover with a lid to keep warm while you prepare the corned beef.

4. Make the spice rub: In a small bowl, combine the ancho chile powder, paprika, oregano, coriander, mustard powder, cumin, chile de árbol powder, salt, and black pepper. Spread the spice rub onto a plate.

Recipe and ingredients continue

Serves 4

3-pound corned beef brisket (spice packet discarded)

Mustard Sauce

¼ cup Dijon mustard

¼ cup whole-grain mustard

¼ cup honey

2 tablespoons prepared horseradish, drained

Kosher salt and freshly ground black pepper

Sweet-and-Sour Cabbage and Kale

3 tablespoons extra-virgin olive oil

½ Spanish onion, thinly sliced

2 garlic cloves, finely chopped to a paste with ½ teaspoon kosher salt

½ small head red cabbage, thinly sliced (about 4 cups)

½ small head green cabbage, thinly sliced (about 4 cups)

Kosher salt and freshly ground black pepper

1 bunch lacinato kale, ribs and stems removed, thinly sliced (about 4 cups)

¾ teaspoon caraway seeds

⅓ cup red wine vinegar

3 tablespoons honey

2 tablespoons unsalted butter

5. Cut the slightly cooled corned beef crosswise into 8 even pieces, each about ¾ inch thick. Dredge one side of each slice of corned beef in the rub and tap off the excess.

6. In a large cast-iron skillet, heat 2 tablespoons of the neutral oil over medium-high heat until it begins to shimmer. Add half of the cooked, sliced corned beef, rub side down, and cook until a golden-brown crust has formed, about 2 minutes. Flip the slices and continue cooking until golden, 1 to 2 minutes longer. Transfer to a baking sheet and repeat with the remaining corned beef slices and 2 tablespoons neutral oil.

7. Spoon the cabbage and kale onto a serving platter and place the corned beef slices on top. Serve immediately with the mustard sauce on the side.

Spice Rub

1½ tablespoons ancho chile powder

1 tablespoon Spanish sweet paprika

1½ teaspoons dried oregano

1½ teaspoons ground coriander

1½ teaspoons mustard powder

½ teaspoon ground cumin

½ teaspoon chile de árbol powder

½ teaspoon kosher salt

½ teaspoon freshly ground black pepper

4 tablespoons neutral oil, such as avocado or canola

Steak Ranchero
with Red Chile Butter

I love this steak dish for Sunday night dinner because it's really just a bunch of ingredients—tomato, grilled onion, charred chiles, and a smoky red chile butter—all tossed together and scattered over a charred, juicy steak. Serve it with a side of tortillas if you're in a taco mood.

1. In a food processor, combine the butter, pureed chipotle, and ½ teaspoon of the garlic and season with salt and pepper. Blend until smooth. Transfer to a small bowl and set aside.

2. In a shallow baking dish, stir together ¼ cup of the olive oil, the remaining garlic, the lime juice, orange juice, onion powder, guajillo chile powder, and ancho chile powder. Add the flank steak and turn to coat well in the marinade. Cover and refrigerate for at least 30 minutes and up to 2 hours.

3. Remove the steak from the refrigerator 30 minutes before cooking, to take the chill off. Preheat a charcoal or gas grill to high.

4. Line a large plate or baking sheet with paper towels. Remove the steak from the marinade, allow any excess marinade to drip off, then gently pat the steak with paper towels to wipe away the excess moisture. Season on both sides with salt and pepper and transfer to the lined plate or baking sheet.

5. Grill the steak until charred on both sides and cooked to medium-rare doneness, 5 to 7 minutes per side. Remove from the grill and slather the top of the steak with some of the red chile butter. Let the steak rest while you grill the vegetables.

6. Brush the Roma tomato, Fresno chiles, and sliced red onion rounds with the remaining 1 tablespoon oil and season with salt and pepper. Add the vegetables to the grill and cook until charred in spots and tender, 2 to 4 minutes for the tomato, 3 to 5 minutes for the chiles, and 6 to 8 minutes for the onion.

7. Remove the vegetables from the grill as they finish cooking and thinly slice the chiles and coarsely chop the tomato and onion. Thinly slice the rested steak against the grain and slather with any remaining red chile butter. Transfer to a platter, top with the grilled vegetables, and garnish with chopped cilantro. Serve immediately with lime wedges and warm tortillas (if using) on the side.

Serves 4

1 stick (4 ounces) unsalted butter, at room temperature

1 tablespoon pureed canned chipotle pepper in adobo sauce

3 garlic cloves, finely chopped to a paste with ¼ teaspoon kosher salt

Kosher salt and freshly ground black pepper

¼ cup plus 1 tablespoon extra-virgin olive oil

3 tablespoons fresh lime juice

⅓ cup fresh orange juice

2 teaspoons onion powder

1 tablespoon guajillo chile powder (or another good-quality red chile powder of your choice)

1 tablespoon ancho chile powder

2-pound flank steak

1 Roma tomato, halved

3 Fresno chiles

1 red onion, cut into rounds ½ inch thick

Chopped fresh cilantro leaves, for garnish

Lime wedges, for serving

Corn or flour tortillas, warmed, for serving (optional)

Red Wine–Braised Short Ribs

Serves 4

This is classic fall or winter cooking. Lots of red wine, vegetables, and the anticipation of succulent, falling-off-the-bone beef cozied up next to some risotto, polenta, egg noodles, or mashed potatoes—anything starchy and comforting. The flavor is all in the reduced braising broth. It really is liquid gold, so take the time to cook it low and slow. Any leftovers are great in tacos: I like to fold some pureed chipotles in adobo into the sauce for rich smokiness and a little fire, then spoon the short ribs onto a tortilla and top with crunchy pickled onions and velvety avocado.

1. Set an oven rack in the middle position and preheat the oven to 375°F.

2. Season the short ribs generously with salt and pepper. In a large Dutch oven, heat the neutral oil over medium-high heat until it starts to shimmer. Add the short ribs and cook until deeply browned on all sides, about 15 minutes total. Transfer the ribs to a baking sheet.

3. Add the onion, celery, and carrots to the Dutch oven. Cook, stirring occasionally, until the vegetables are lightly browned and softened, about 10 minutes. Add the garlic and cook until soft, about 1 minute. Add the brown sugar and tomato paste, stir to combine, and cook for 2 minutes. Add the flour and cook for 1 minute.

4. Add the wine and use a wooden spoon to scrape up any browned bits at the bottom of the Dutch oven. Add the chicken stock, black peppercorns, fennel seeds, and thyme. Add enough water so that the vegetables are covered by 3 inches.

5. Return the short ribs to the Dutch oven, cover, and cook in the oven until the short ribs are very tender, about 3 hours. Turn off the oven. Remove the ribs from the cooking liquid and place on a baking sheet, cover with foil, and return to the turned-off oven to keep warm. Strain the braising liquid into a large saucepan and discard the vegetables.

6. Skim any excess fat from the braising liquid, then bring to a boil over medium-high heat. Reduce the heat to medium for a strong simmer and cook, stirring occasionally, until the mixture is reduced by half, about 25 minutes. Season with salt and pepper.

7. Arrange the short ribs on a large platter and spoon the sauce over the ribs. Garnish with fresh thyme leaves and serve.

3 pounds bone-in beef short ribs (5 or 6 ribs)

Kosher salt and freshly ground black pepper

2 tablespoons neutral oil, such as avocado or canola

1 medium Spanish onion, diced

2 celery stalks, diced

3 large carrots, diced

6 garlic cloves, lightly smashed

1 tablespoon light brown sugar

3 tablespoons tomato paste

1 tablespoon all-purpose flour

3 cups dry red wine

4 cups chicken stock, homemade (page 243) or store-bought

2 teaspoons black peppercorns

1 tablespoon fennel seeds

6 sprigs thyme, plus more leaves for garnish

Cast-Iron Steak
with Butter and Cremini Mushrooms

Serves 4

2 (1½-pound) bone-in rib eye steaks, 1½ to 2 inches thick

Kosher salt and freshly ground black pepper

2 tablespoons neutral oil, such as avocado or canola

1 stick (4 ounces) unsalted butter, cut into tablespoons (6 tablespoons at room temperature and 2 tablespoons cold)

2 tablespoons extra-virgin olive oil

10 ounces cremini mushrooms, quartered (about 5 cups)

1 teaspoon finely chopped fresh thyme leaves

2 garlic cloves, finely chopped to a paste with ¼ teaspoon kosher salt

⅔ cup dry white wine

2 tablespoons chopped fresh flat-leaf parsley leaves

If you've read my other books, you'll know that I have a very particular steak technique that I learned many years ago at the great Peter Luger steakhouse in Brooklyn, New York. Their technique of searing, slicing, and then finishing a steak under the broiler really stuck with me, and now it's hard to get me to cook a rib eye any other way. Let the butter melt, hit the bottom of the pan, and get a little nutty brown. So good.

1. Remove the steaks from the refrigerator 30 minutes before cooking and season very generously with salt and pepper. Preheat the broiler.

2. In a large cast-iron skillet, heat the neutral oil over medium-high heat until it begins to shimmer. Add 1 steak and cook until a deep brown crust forms on the bottom, 3 to 4 minutes. Turn the steak and cook until the second side is deeply browned, about 3 minutes longer. Transfer the steak to a cutting board. Add the second steak and repeat the cooking process. Transfer the second steak to the cutting board. Remove the skillet from the heat and carefully pour the used oil into a small heatproof bowl (once cooled, discard the oil).

3. Cut the meat off the bone (1 whole piece per steak), then slice both steaks against the grain 1 inch thick. Reassemble the sliced steaks around the bone and return both to the skillet. Top with the 6 tablespoons of room temperature butter.

4. Transfer the cast-iron skillet to the broiler and cook, occasionally spooning some of the butter on top, until the steaks are cooked to medium-rare, 2 to 5 minutes. Transfer both steaks to a cutting board. Pour the butter and pan juices from the skillet into a small bowl and set aside.

5. In the same skillet, heat the olive oil over medium-high heat until it begins to shimmer. Add the mushrooms and cook, stirring occasionally, until they are golden brown, about 8 minutes. Reduce the heat to medium, add the thyme and garlic, and cook for 1 minute. Add the wine and cook until reduced by half, about 2 minutes. Add the 2 tablespoons of cold butter, 1 at a time, stirring well after each addition. Season to taste with salt and pepper and stir in the parsley.

6. Transfer the steaks to a serving platter, top with the mushrooms, and drizzle with some of the reserved butter and pan juices. Serve immediately.

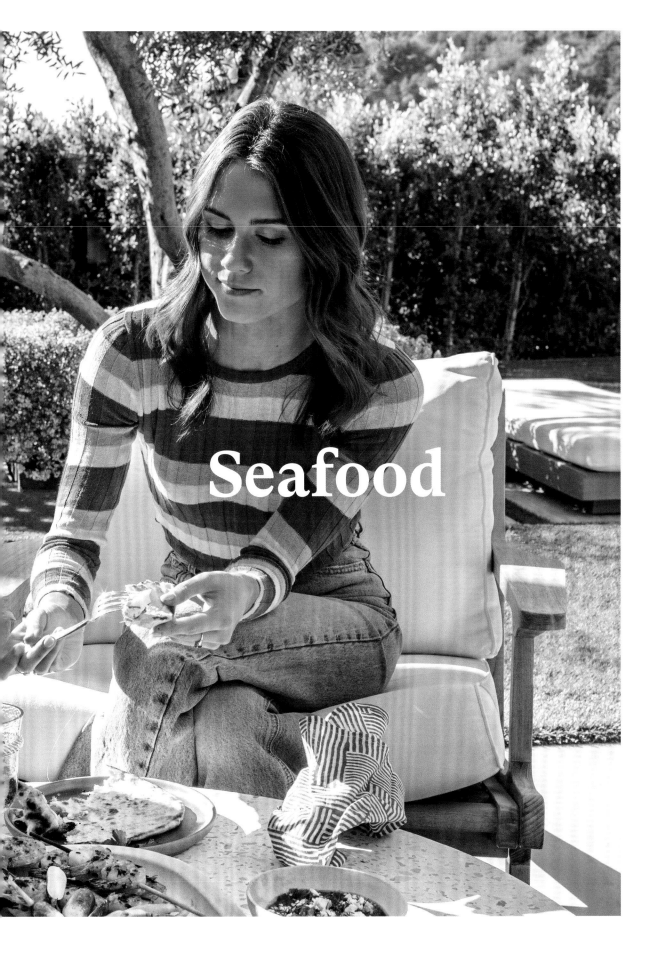

Seafood

Steamed Mussels
Da Adolfo Style

Da Adolfo is the seafood shack of my dreams, nestled in a cove on the Amalfi Coast near the town of Positano. Da Adolfo is known for a handful of classic regional dishes, none more popular than their mussels. They're steamed with white wine and tomato and I'm sure a touch of Italian butter. My version might not be exactly what they do, but it's always a crowd-pleaser and so easy to prepare.

1. In a large Dutch oven, heat the olive oil over medium-high heat until it begins to shimmer. Add the shallots, season with salt and black pepper, and cook until soft, about 5 minutes. Add the garlic and cook until soft, about 30 seconds.

2. Add the tomato puree, wine, and pepper flakes and bring to a boil. Stir in the mussels, making sure they are coated with the tomato puree and shallots. Cover and cook until all the mussels have opened, about 5 minutes. Remove the mussels with a slotted spoon and transfer to a large shallow bowl. (Discard any that have not opened.)

3. Bring the cooking liquid back to a boil and begin whisking in the cold butter, piece by piece, until the sauce begins to thicken, about 2 minutes. Stir in the parsley and season with salt and pepper. Pour the broth over the mussels and garnish with additional parsley. Serve immediately with the toasted ciabatta.

Serves 2 to 3 as an appetizer

2 tablespoons extra-virgin olive oil

2 large shallots, finely diced

Kosher salt and freshly ground black pepper

3 garlic cloves, finely chopped to a paste with ¼ teaspoon kosher salt

1 cup tomato puree

1 cup dry white wine

¼ teaspoon red pepper flakes

3 pounds mussels, scrubbed and debearded

4 tablespoons cold unsalted butter, cut into tablespoons

2 tablespoons chopped fresh flat-leaf parsley leaves, plus more for garnish

Toasted ciabatta bread, for serving

> **❝**
>
> My dad loves to tell the story of when I was a baby, and he had to warn the staff at his restaurants Mesa and Bolo not to leave a bowl of steamed mussels near me. If they did, as soon as they turned around I would pull the mussels out of the shells and eat them, one by one. Even if the mussels were intended for some other guest. I was just a baby obsessed with steamed mussels. —SF
>
> **❞**

Grilled Lobster
with Ginger-Soy Butter

Serves 4

¼ cup **soy sauce**

Finely grated zest and juice of 1 **lime**

2 **garlic cloves,** finely grated

2-inch piece fresh **ginger,** peeled and finely grated

1½ sticks (6 ounces) **unsalted butter,** at room temperature

Kosher salt and freshly ground **black pepper**

2 tablespoons sliced **scallions,** plus more for garnish

4 (2-pound) **whole lobsters**

Neutral oil, such as avocado or canola, for brushing

Sophie's never met a lobster she didn't like, so lobsters show up in my home cooking a lot. During the summer, I love to cook them on the grill. Where there is grilled lobster there must be some sort of butter. Drawn (aka clarified) butter is the classic, but I always find it to be less satisfying than I hoped it would be. So why not pump some flavor into it with fresh ginger, garlic, and soy sauce? I've been known to make basil butter or red chile butter as well.

1. In a food processor, combine the soy sauce, lime zest, lime juice, garlic, ginger, and butter. Pulse until thoroughly combined and smooth. Season with salt and pepper and pulse again. Transfer to a bowl, fold in the sliced scallions, and set aside.

2. Set up a large container (big enough to hold 4 lobsters) with ice and water. Bring a large pot of salted water to a boil. Working in batches as needed, boil the lobsters, covered, for 6 to 8 minutes. They will be three-quarters done. Remove the lobsters from the pot and put directly into the ice water bath. Once the lobsters are completely cooled, drain well. Cut each lobster in half lengthwise and remove any of the innards at the top of the lobster bodies.

3. Preheat a charcoal or gas grill to high heat. Brush the cut side of the lobsters with some oil and sprinkle with salt and pepper. Grill, cut side down, until slightly charred, about 2 minutes. Flip and continue grilling until lightly charred and heated through, about 2 minutes. Transfer the lobsters from the grill to a large platter.

4. Slather the lobsters with the ginger-soy butter, garnish with additional sliced scallions, and serve immediately.

— **❝** —

My dad taught me the real trick to eating lobsters, which is to not only eat all the tail and claw meat but also the meat from the legs. When it comes to lobster, you don't want to leave behind a single bite. —SF

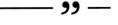

Shrimp Mezze Platter

with Spicy Tomato Sauce, Pesto-Swirled Yogurt,
and White Bean Hummus

I love eating this way: mezze-style, with plenty of small plates like dips, veg, and pita to share at the table. What's great about communal, Mediterranean-style feasts like this is that they're packed with flavor and all sorts of contrasting textures—juicy grilled shrimp, spicy tomato, rich and tangy yogurt, white beans spun into a savory hummus—but still very healthy. This platter and a glass or two of rosé? Sign me up all summer.

1. Soak five 10-inch wooden skewers in water for 30 minutes.

2. Make the shrimp: In a medium bowl, combine the lemon juice, olive oil, garlic, oregano, and shrimp and stir to coat the shrimp. Thread the shrimp onto the soaked skewers (figure 4 shrimp per skewer) so that the skewers go through the tail and thick end of each shrimp. Transfer the skewers to a baking sheet and spoon any extra marinade onto the shrimp.

3. Preheat a charcoal or gas grill to high heat. Season the shrimp on all sides with salt and pepper. Grill until lightly golden brown on both sides and opaque, 1 to 2 minutes per side. Transfer the grilled shrimp skewers to a large platter.

4. For serving: In a small saucepan, bring the tomato sauce to a simmer over medium heat. Add the chile de árbol powder and cook, stirring occasionally, for 5 minutes. Season with salt and pepper. Add the hot tomato sauce to a serving bowl, top with the feta cheese, and garnish with chopped dill.

5. In a medium serving bowl, season the Greek yogurt with salt and pepper. Use the back of a spoon to swirl the pesto into the yogurt. Drizzle with olive oil.

6. Place the hummus in a separate serving bowl, drizzle with oil, and garnish with chopped parsley.

7. Set out the platter of grilled shrimp alongside the spicy tomato sauce, yogurt with shishito pesto, hummus, grilled pita bread, and your favorite crunchy raw vegetables.

Serves 4 to 6

Shrimp

1 tablespoon fresh lemon juice

¼ cup extra-virgin olive oil

3 garlic cloves, finely chopped to a paste with ¼ teaspoon kosher salt

1 tablespoon chopped fresh oregano leaves

1 pound extra-large (16/20 count) shrimp, peeled and deveined, tail on

Kosher salt and freshly ground black pepper

For Serving

1½ cups Basic Tomato Sauce (page 243)

⅛ teaspoon chile de árbol powder or cayenne pepper, or more to taste

Kosher salt and freshly ground black pepper

1 ounce feta cheese, crumbled

Chopped fresh dill, for garnish

1 cup 2% plain Greek yogurt

½ cup Shishito Pesto (page 244)

Extra-virgin olive oil, for drizzling

White Bean Hummus (page 247)

Chopped fresh flat-leaf parsley leaves, for garnish

Grilled pita bread

Fresh vegetables (such as small lettuce leaves, radishes, and cucumbers)

Spicy Thai-Style Green Curry
with Shrimp

I always have cans of Maesri brand Thai green and red curry paste in my pantry. Always. It makes throwing together a last-minute meal pretty easy because the curry pastes have tons of aromatics like garlic, ginger, and chiles and can spice up any protein. Different curry pastes have different heat levels, so if you're using something other than Maesri, you might need to dial up or down the amount of paste you use. For this recipe I'm using shrimp, but any fish, shellfish, or even chicken will work. (Just cut your protein into bite-size pieces and add them when you'd add the shrimp.) Oh, one more thing: Make sure you have one can of full-fat coconut milk for every can of curry in your cupboard. They go hand in hand.

Serves 4

3 tablespoons neutral oil, such as avocado or canola

1 pound extra-large (16/20 count) shrimp, peeled and deveined (shells reserved for stock), tail on

Kosher salt

2 large shallots, finely diced

4 garlic cloves, grated (about 1 tablespoon)

1 tablespoon grated fresh ginger

¼ cup green curry paste (I like Maesri brand)

1½ cups Shrimp Stock (page 243)

1 (13.5-ounce) can full-fat coconut milk, well stirred (about 1¾ cups)

Pinch of sugar

1 tablespoon fish sauce

1 scallion, thinly sliced

¼ cup coarsely chopped fresh cilantro leaves, for garnish

Lime wedges, for serving

Fluffy Rice with Herbs and Lime Zest (recipe follows), Crispy Rice with Tamarind and Coconut (page 79), or cooked jasmine rice, for serving

1. In a large deep skillet, heat the neutral oil over medium-high heat until it shimmers. Season the shrimp on both sides with salt. Add the shrimp to the pan in an even layer and sear until just opaque and golden on both sides, but not cooked through, about 3 minutes. Transfer the shrimp to a plate.

2. Add the shallots and cook until soft, 2 to 3 minutes. Add the garlic and ginger and cook for 1 minute. Add the green curry paste and cook, stirring constantly, until the color deepens and the rawness of the paste is cooked out, 2 to 4 minutes.

3. Add the shrimp stock, coconut milk, sugar, and fish sauce. Bring to a boil, then reduce to a simmer and cook until the curry has thickened slightly and the flavors have melded, 15 to 20 minutes. Add the shrimp and any juices that collected on the plate back to the pan and let simmer, stirring occasionally, until the shrimp are opaque throughout, about 1 minute.

4. Transfer the shrimp curry to four individual serving bowls and top with the scallion and cilantro. Serve with lime wedges and rice.

Fluffy Rice with Herbs and Lime Zest

Makes about 6 cups

1½ cups **basmati rice**
1 tablespoon **extra-virgin olive oil**
1 large **shallot,** finely chopped
2 **garlic cloves,** finely chopped to a paste with ¼ teaspoon **kosher salt**
Kosher salt
Finely grated zest of 2 **limes**
2 tablespoons packed chopped fresh **basil leaves,** plus more for garnish
2 tablespoons packed chopped fresh **mint leaves,** plus more for garnish
Freshly ground **black pepper**

1. Place the rice in a fine-mesh sieve and rinse the rice until the water runs clear. Set the sieve over a bowl to catch excess water and set aside.

2. In a large saucepan, heat the olive oil over medium-high heat. Add the shallot and cook until soft and browned in spots, about 2 minutes. Add the garlic and cook until soft, about 30 seconds. Add 2½ cups water and 1½ teaspoons salt and bring to a boil.

3. Stir in the rice and allow it to come back to a full boil. Reduce the heat to low, cover with a lid, and cook until the rice is tender and all the water has been absorbed, 12 to 15 minutes. Remove the saucepan from the heat and allow the rice to sit for another 5 minutes.

4. Transfer the rice to a large serving bowl. Gently fold in the lime zest, basil, and mint. Season with salt and pepper. Garnish with additional chopped basil and mint and serve immediately.

Swordfish Piccata

with Yellow Tomatoes and Extra Capers

Serves 4

6 tablespoons **unsalted butter**

½ cup **Wondra flour**

Kosher salt and freshly ground **black pepper**

4 (4- to 6-ounce) skinless **swordfish steaks,** ½ inch thick

Kosher salt and freshly ground **black pepper**

1 tablespoon **neutral oil,** such as avocado or canola

1½ cups **yellow cherry tomatoes,** halved

¼ cup **capers,** drained

½ cup **dry white wine**

2 tablespoons fresh **lemon juice**

1 tablespoon chopped fresh **flat-leaf parsley leaves,** plus more for garnish

Lemon wedges, for serving

Piccata anything is always a winner. Chicken, pork, even swordfish. In Italian cooking, the term *piccata* refers to the process of slicing or pounding a piece of meat so it's flat and thin. But in my mind, piccata is all about that sauce of lemon, capers, white wine, and butter . . . game over. I always have to double down on the capers when I make this for Sophie. When she was two years old, she would sit on my lap and eat the capers off my plate one by one. She still requests extra capers whenever they show up in my cooking.

1. Cut 2 tablespoons of the butter into small cubes and chill in the refrigerator. Set aside the remaining 4 tablespoons butter. Put the flour in a shallow bowl or plate and season with salt and pepper.

2. Season the swordfish on both sides with salt and pepper. Dredge in the seasoned flour, shake off any excess, and transfer to a baking sheet.

3. Set a wire rack over a baking sheet. In a large skillet, heat the neutral oil over medium-high heat until it shimmers. Add 2 tablespoons of the room temperature butter. When the butter just starts to brown, add 2 of the dredged swordfish steaks to the skillet and cook until golden brown and just cooked through, about 2 minutes per side. Transfer to the wire rack. Add 1 additional tablespoon of butter to the skillet and cook the remaining 2 steaks. Transfer the steaks to a plate and set aside.

4. Remove the skillet from the heat and carefully pour the used oil and butter into a heatproof bowl (once cooled, discard the fats). Return the skillet to medium-high heat. Add the remaining 1 tablespoon room temperature butter to the skillet and melt. Add the cherry tomatoes and capers and cook until some of the tomatoes just start to soften, about 1 minute.

5. Add the wine to the skillet and cook until reduced by half, 2 to 3 minutes. Add the lemon juice, cook for 1 minute, then remove the pan from the heat. Add the cubes of cold butter, 1 or 2 at a time, stirring well after each addition. Stir in the parsley. Season to taste with salt and pepper if needed.

6. Transfer the fish to a large platter or divide among four plates and top with the sauce. Garnish with additional chopped parsley and serve immediately with lemon wedges.

Piccata Anything

Bobby

An easy way to get Sophie excited about a dish is to throw capers in it. Here the capers become the star of a delicious pan sauce that gets poured over whatever protein you have on hand—it could be a piece of chicken or a fillet of fish. A pan sauce is a basic French technique and just what it sounds like: a sauce prepared in the same pan you used to cook the protein. All you need is some white wine to deglaze the pan and get all those flavorful bits that have stuck to the bottom; fresh lemon juice, lime juice, or vinegar for additional acidity; some chopped fresh herbs like parsley or cilantro to lend some brightness; unsalted butter to emulsify the sauce; and if you're me or Sophie, briny capers just because we love them. Here are the rules to a good pan sauce.

Sophie

My dad is the king of capers. I swear, he practically carries capers around with him in his back pocket. I love them, too—I could throw back a jar of capers, no problem—but I definitely inherited it from him. Whenever I envision him cooking fish, it's either with Shishito Pesto (page 244), romesco sauce (from Panfried Asparagus with Romesco and Pecorino, page 211), or a crazy amount of capers. Come to think of it, he loves capers with chicken and pork, too. We're clearly related.

Scrape up the browned bits. Once you've finished cooking your protein, remove it from the pan but keep the pan on the heat. While the pan is still hot, add some wine and simmer until it reduces and the alcohol cooks away. Using a wooden spoon, help nudge the flavorful bits on the bottom of the pan to release and become part of the sauce.

Use cold butter. Cold butter melts slowly, which allows its fat content to bind to the reduced wine and lemon juice and act as a thickening agent. This helps create a silky sauce.

Add acid. Everyone always talks about how important salt is in cooking. But I'd argue acid is equally important. Try a squeeze of fresh lemon, tart tomatoes, dry white wine, or a nice vinegar. It's essential for any good sauce.

Harissa-Glazed Striped Bass

Serves 4

I love using harissa because it has so many layers of flavors and well-balanced ingredients. Using it as a base for a sauce or a glaze almost feels like cheating, because the depth and complexity are already there. In the summer I eat wild striped bass more than any other fish because it's caught in the waters off Montauk, less than fifteen miles from where I live. When Sophie convinces me that we need to cook some fish for lunch, this dish is definitely one of my faves—it's great to feed a crowd. Sophie usually makes a side dish to go with it . . . Just kidding. She opens the rosé!

1. Set an oven rack in the middle position and preheat the oven to 425°F. Line a large sheet pan with parchment paper and set aside.

2. In a small bowl, combine 1½ teaspoons salt, ½ teaspoon pepper, and the guajillo chile powder. Stir to combine and set aside.

3. In a second small bowl, combine the mustard, honey, horseradish, vinegar, and harissa paste. Whisk the harissa glaze until smooth.

4. Lay the fillets top side up on the lined pan. Brush the fish all over with the olive oil, then season with the guajillo/salt mixture. Lightly brush some of the harissa glaze onto the top of the fillets.

5. Roast in the oven, basting with additional glaze occasionally, until the fish is just cooked through and opaque in the center, 12 to 18 minutes, depending on the thickness of the fish.

6. Remove the fish from the oven, brush more glaze on top, and allow the fish to rest while you make the herb salad.

7. In a small bowl, combine the dill, cilantro, parsley, and lime zest. Season with salt and pepper. Toss to combine.

8. Transfer the fish to a large platter, top with the herb salad, and drizzle with additional oil. Serve immediately.

Kosher salt and freshly ground black pepper

1½ teaspoons guajillo chile powder (or another good-quality red chile powder of your choice)

1 tablespoon whole-grain mustard

1 tablespoon honey

1 tablespoon prepared horseradish, drained

2 tablespoons white wine vinegar

2 tablespoons harissa paste

4 (6-ounce) skinless striped bass fillets

1 tablespoon extra-virgin olive oil, plus more for drizzling

1 tablespoon lightly packed coarsely chopped fresh dill

1 tablespoon lightly packed cilantro leaves

1 tablespoon lightly packed flat-leaf parsley leaves

Finely grated zest of 1 lime

Pan-Seared Halibut
with Corn-Curry Sauce

This is not a new dish for me—I've been cooking it for years. But one day I realized I'd never made it for Sophie and I needed to put it on her radar. I'll just set the scene for you: silky, flaky, and pristine-tasting fish nestled in a bath of creamy, golden corn broth, speckled with spices, and all tied together with coconut milk and bright herbs. It's spicy, sweet, and rich.

Serves 4

3 large ears yellow corn, husked

½ Spanish onion, coarsely chopped

1 celery stalk, coarsely chopped

1 bay leaf

1 tablespoon plus 1½ teaspoons extra-virgin olive oil

Kosher salt and freshly ground black pepper

1 jalapeño, seeded (optional) and finely diced

2 tablespoons sliced scallions

¼ cup chopped fresh cilantro leaves

Finely grated zest and juice of 1 lime

3 tablespoons neutral oil, such as avocado or canola

1 large shallot, finely diced

2 garlic cloves, grated

1 tablespoon grated fresh ginger

2 teaspoons Madras hot curry powder

½ cup dry white wine

¾ cup canned full-fat coconut milk, well stirred

4 (6-ounce) skinless halibut fillets, preferably center cut

1. Cut the kernels off the corn cobs, then place the cobs and ¼ cup of the kernels into a large saucepan. Add the onion, celery, bay leaf, and 2½ cups water. Bring to a boil over medium-high heat, then reduce to a simmer and cook for 30 minutes.

2. Pour the broth through a fine-mesh sieve set over a large bowl, pressing down on the solids until all the liquid has been extracted (discard the solids). You should have about 1½ cups of broth. If not, add enough water to bring the total to 1½ cups. Set the corn broth aside.

3. In a small sauté pan, heat 1½ teaspoons of the olive oil over medium-high heat. Add 1 cup of the corn, season with salt and pepper, and cook until tender and browned in spots, 2 to 4 minutes. Transfer to a medium bowl to cool completely.

4. Add the jalapeño, scallions, half of the cilantro, the lime zest and juice, and remaining 1 tablespoon olive oil to the cooled corn. Season with salt and pepper, stir to combine, and set the corn relish aside.

5. In the same saucepan that you used to make the broth, heat 1 tablespoon of the neutral oil over medium heat. Add the shallot and cook, stirring constantly, until soft, about 5 minutes. Add the garlic, ginger, and remaining corn and season with salt and pepper. Cook, stirring occasionally, for 2 minutes, then add the curry powder and cook, stirring constantly, for 1 minute.

6. Add the wine, increase the heat to medium-high, and cook until almost completely evaporated, about 3 minutes, scraping up any browned bits at the bottom of the pan. Add the reserved corn broth and cook, adjusting the heat to maintain a simmer, until reduced by about half, about 5 minutes.

7. Add the coconut milk and season with salt and pepper. Simmer until the curry sauce has reduced slightly and the flavors have melded, about 10 minutes. Season with salt and pepper. Transfer the mixture to a blender. Remove the steam vent from the center of the lid, cover the small opening with a kitchen towel (this will help to release steam), and blend until smooth.

8. Set a fine-mesh sieve over the saucepan you cooked the sauce in and strain the sauce through the sieve. Use the back of a spoon to help push down on the solids (discard the solids). The sauce should be thick but pourable. If needed, stir in additional water, 1 tablespoon at a time, until you achieve the desired consistency. Cover with a lid and keep warm on low heat while you cook the halibut.

9. Set an oven rack in the middle position and preheat the oven to 400°F.

10. Season the halibut on all sides with salt and pepper. In a large cast-iron skillet or other ovenproof skillet, heat the remaining 2 tablespoons neutral oil over medium-high heat until it starts to shimmer. Add the halibut and cook until deeply seared on the first side, 2 to 4 minutes. Flip and cook until deeply seared on the second side, 2 to 4 minutes longer. Transfer the skillet to the oven and roast until the fish is just cooked through and opaque in the center, 3 to 5 minutes longer (depending on the thickness of the fish).

11. Stir the remaining cilantro into the corn-curry sauce and spoon the sauce into four shallow serving bowls. Nestle the halibut into the sauce, then top with the corn relish. Serve immediately.

Slow-Roasted Salmon
with Arugula Pesto and Seared Lemon

Serves 4 to 6

2-pound skinless salmon fillet, preferably center cut

2 tablespoons fresh lemon juice plus 1 lemon, halved crosswise

2 tablespoons fresh orange juice

3 tablespoons extra-virgin olive oil

Kosher salt and freshly ground black pepper

½ teaspoon neutral oil, such as avocado or canola

1 cup Arugula Pesto (page 244)

Fresh flat-leaf parsley leaves, for garnish

I recently taught Sophie my favorite way to cook salmon, which is to roast it in a low oven rather than blasting it at a high temp. The result is so buttery and delicious. I try to make a pesto out of pretty much any green or herb I come across. Arugula works well here because of its pepperiness, which balances the richness of the fish.

1. Set an oven rack in the middle position and preheat the oven to 275°F.

2. Place the salmon in a large baking dish. In a small bowl, whisk together the lemon juice, orange juice, and olive oil. Season the salmon on both sides with salt and pepper, then brush liberally with the citrus juice/olive oil mixture. Turn the fish so it is top side up and pour the remaining citrus juice/olive oil mixture over the fish.

3. Roast in the oven until the fish is buttery and soft and a thermometer inserted in the thickest portion reads 140°F, about 45 minutes (depending on the thickness of the fish), spooning the olive oil and citrus juice in the baking dish over the salmon every 10 to 15 minutes.

4. Meanwhile, heat a small cast-iron skillet over high heat. Cut the ends off the lemon halves so that they sit flat and brush the cut sides with the neutral oil. Place the lemons cut side down into the hot skillet and sear until deeply charred, about 5 minutes. Do not move the lemon halves during this process and use the back of a flat spatula to periodically press down on the lemons as they sear. Transfer the lemons to a small plate and set aside.

5. Once the fish is roasted, allow it to rest in the baking dish for 5 minutes. Use a large flat spatula to carefully transfer the fish to a large platter. Spoon some of the juices from the baking dish over the fish and around the platter. Nestle the seared lemon halves next to the salmon, top the fish with some of the arugula pesto, and garnish with parsley leaves. Serve immediately with any remaining arugula pesto on the side.

A New Way with Salmon

Bobby

A lot of people approach salmon the same way they do other fish, like tuna: They cook it quickly in a hot oven. That gets you a good sear, but I don't really like salmon that's rare in the middle and seared on top. Some fish are good like that—tuna, for example—but salmon just isn't one of them. Instead, I recommend you go low and slow.

Embrace the salmon's natural fattiness.
Salmon has an amazing amount of its own fat—healthy omega-3s—and when you cook it low and slow, you're essentially melting that fat and allowing it to baste the salmon meat as it cooks. Sort of like a fish version of confit. This means you don't even have to add much additional cooking fat—a little olive oil will do the trick.

Don't obsess over the internal temp. The nice thing about the low-and-slow approach is, since you're not shooting for rare, you have a bit of a cushion when it comes to doneness.

Balance it out with acid and herbs. As with any rich dish, you're going to need some acid to cut through the fat. Citrus and fresh herbs or greens like parsley and arugula are a great pairing.

Sophie

Typically when I'm cooking, I rely on recipes I find online. My dad always makes fun of me about it—"Your father is a professional chef! Why are you using recipes from TikTok?" There are definitely moments when he's been proven right. For example, I always used to cook salmon the way most online recipes tell you to do it: in a 400°F oven for 10 minutes. Too often, I'd end up with dry, sad salmon. Until my dad taught me his slow-roasted method. I remember the first time I tasted it. I asked him, "How much butter did you put on this? It tastes so rich and buttery." And he assured me that he hadn't used any butter at all, just a drizzle of olive oil. But he had roasted it on lower heat for longer. Now I will never make salmon any other way. It's so delicious like this.

Salads

Roasted Portobello Salad
with Pecorino

Serves 4

4 **portobello mushrooms,** stems removed

¼ cup plus 2 tablespoons **extra-virgin olive oil**

Kosher salt and freshly ground **black pepper**

1 teaspoon chopped fresh **thyme leaves**

2 teaspoons **Dijon mustard**

3 tablespoons **red wine vinegar**

1 teaspoon **honey**

1 small **shallot,** minced

4 cups lightly packed **baby arugula** (about 4 ounces)

1 small **fennel bulb,** halved and very thinly sliced (about 1½ cups)

1 ounce **Pecorino Romano cheese,** thinly shaved

¼ cup hand-torn fresh **mint leaves**

I always have some variety of mushroom rolling around my refrigerator. It could be cremini, portobello, oyster, or one of the cool, dramatic-looking varieties like hen of the woods. This dish was inspired by a key lesson my love and obsession with Italian cuisine has taught me: A few simple ingredients can be so satisfying. In this case, I'm roasting a whole portobello cap and using it as a canvas for a salad of arugula, fennel, and some Pecorino Romano, a sheep's milk cheese that has a little bite to it. Feel free to use a good quality Parmigiano if that's what you have. It's a little sweeter in flavor, but it also works.

1. Set an oven rack in the middle position and preheat the oven to 425°F.

2. Line a large baking sheet with parchment paper and add the mushroom caps. Rub the mushrooms on all sides with 2 tablespoons of the olive oil and season with salt and pepper and the thyme. Turn the mushroom caps gills side up and roast until golden brown and tender, about 30 minutes, flipping the mushroom caps over halfway through the cooking time.

3. Meanwhile, in a medium bowl, combine the mustard, vinegar, honey, and shallot and season with salt and pepper. Stream in the remaining ¼ cup oil slowly and whisk quickly to emulsify.

4. In a large bowl, combine the arugula, fennel, half of the Romano and half of the mint. Season with salt and pepper. Drizzle half of the dressing around the sides of the bowl, then use tongs to lightly dress the arugula, fennel, cheese, and mint.

5. Set a whole roasted mushroom cap on each of four serving plates. Drizzle some of the dressing on top and add some salad. Top with the remaining shaved cheese and mint and serve.

Butter Lettuce and Arugula

with Marcona Almonds, Pink Peppercorns, and Asiago

Sometimes I struggle to make salads at home interesting enough to sit at the table with the rest of the dishes. But I liked this one so much, it made it onto my menu at Amalfi in Las Vegas. Everyone should have a classic green salad in their repertoire. I call this my "pink and green salad" because of the delicate pink-skinned radishes and crushed pink peppercorns that contrast with the green butter lettuce and arugula.

1. In a medium bowl, combine the mustard, vinegar, lemon juice, honey, garlic, and shallot and season with salt and pepper. Stream in the olive oil slowly and whisk quickly to emulsify.

2. In a large bowl, combine the butter lettuce (tear any extra-large leaves into bite-size pieces), arugula, radishes, half of the pink peppercorns, half of the almonds, half of the Asiago, and half of the Parmigiano. Season with salt and pepper. Drizzle half of the dressing around the sides of the bowl, then use tongs to lightly dress the salad.

3. Transfer the salad to a large platter, drizzle with the remaining dressing, and top with the remaining pink peppercorns, almonds, Asiago, and Parmigiano. Serve immediately.

Serves 4 to 6

2 teaspoons Dijon mustard

2 tablespoons red wine vinegar

2 tablespoons fresh lemon juice

1½ teaspoons honey

1 garlic clove, finely chopped to a paste with ⅛ teaspoon kosher salt

1 small shallot, minced

Kosher salt and freshly ground black pepper

⅓ cup extra-virgin olive oil

1 head butter lettuce, leaves separated

3 cups lightly packed baby arugula (about 3 ounces)

2 radishes, very thinly sliced

2 teaspoons pink peppercorns, lightly crushed

¼ cup salted roasted Marcona almonds, coarsely chopped

½ cup freshly grated Asiago cheese

1½ ounces Parmigiano-Reggiano cheese, thinly shaved

Baby Gem and Kale Caesar

Serves 4

Baby Gems, better known as Little Gems, are small, crispy versions of romaine lettuce. They're great in a Caesar salad, and I'm a Caesar salad fanatic. Add a big steak, some crusty potatoes, and a bottle of big red wine and it's Steakhouse Night at the Flays'!

1. Preheat the oven to 375°F. Pull the insides from the bread and tear into irregular bite-size pieces. Grate the zest from the lemon, then squeeze the lemon to get 2 tablespoons. Set the juice and zest aside.

2. In a large sauté pan, heat 3 tablespoons of the olive oil over medium-high heat. Add 4 of the garlic cloves and cook until lightly browned (this will lightly flavor the oil), about 3 minutes. Remove from the heat and discard the garlic. Add the torn bread, season with salt, and toss to coat. Transfer the bread to a large baking sheet.

3. Bake the croutons until golden brown and crispy, about 15 minutes, gently stirring the bread once, halfway through the cooking time. Cool completely on the baking sheet.

4. Meanwhile, in a food processor, combine the mayonnaise, mustard, Worcestershire sauce, vinegar, reserved lemon juice, remaining 2 garlic cloves, the anchovies, and ¼ cup of the Parmigiano. Season with salt and pepper and pulse until coarsely chopped. With the food processor running, slowly stream in the remaining 6 tablespoons oil and blend until smooth.

5. In a medium bowl, combine the kale, half of the reserved lemon zest, and 1 tablespoon Parmigiano. Season with salt and pepper. Drizzle 3 tablespoons of dressing around the sides of the bowl, then use tongs to dress the kale. Let the kale sit at room temperature, tossing a few times, for at least 15 minutes and up to 30 minutes to soften it slightly.

6. Once the kale is softened, add half of the croutons and fold together. In another bowl, combine the Treviso, Baby Gem lettuce, remaining lemon zest, and 1 tablespoon of the Parmigiano. Season with salt and pepper, drizzle 3 tablespoons of dressing around the sides of the bowl, then use tongs to dress the greens.

7. Put the Treviso and Baby Gem lettuce on one side of a large serving platter. Add the kale and croutons to the other side of the platter. Drizzle with the remaining dressing and top with the remaining croutons and Parmigiano. Serve immediately.

4 ounces country loaf (enough to yield about 2 cups of croutons)

1 lemon

9 tablespoons extra-virgin olive oil

6 garlic cloves, lightly smashed

Kosher salt

1 tablespoon mayonnaise

1 teaspoon Dijon mustard

½ teaspoon Worcestershire sauce

1 tablespoon white wine vinegar

2 oil-packed anchovy fillets

½ cup freshly grated Parmigiano-Reggiano cheese

Freshly ground black pepper

1 small bunch lacinato kale, ribs and stems removed, cut into bite-size pieces

1 small head Treviso, leaves separated

1 head Baby Gem lettuce (or romaine heart), leaves separated

Baby Gems and Radicchio
with Goat Cheese, Pistachios, and Cranberries

Serves 4

1 cup freshly squeezed orange juice

2 tablespoons fresh lime juice

2 teaspoons Dijon mustard

1 teaspoon honey

1 small shallot, minced

Kosher salt and freshly ground black pepper

½ cup extra-virgin olive oil

½ small head radicchio, leaves separated

3 heads Baby Gem lettuce, leaves separated

¼ cup salted roasted pistachios, coarsely chopped

¼ cup dried cranberries

2 ounces goat cheese, crumbled

I love this dish for the fall. In fact, it would be a terrific Thanksgiving salad. The lettuce and radicchio are crisp and slightly bitter, but the most interesting part to me is the combination of goat cheese, pistachios, and cranberries. It's creamy, crunchy, and fruity. What more can you want from a salad? I mean, it's a salad.

1. In a medium saucepan, bring the orange juice to a boil over medium-high heat. Reduce the heat to a strong simmer and cook until the liquid is reduced to ¼ cup, about 20 minutes. Transfer to a large bowl and cool completely.

2. Add the lime juice, mustard, honey, and shallot to the orange juice reduction. Season with salt and pepper. Stream in the olive oil slowly and whisk quickly to emulsify.

3. Tear the radicchio leaves into roughly 1-inch pieces and add to a large bowl. Add the Baby Gem lettuce, 2 tablespoons of the pistachios, and 3 tablespoons of the cranberries. Season with salt and pepper, drizzle ⅓ cup of dressing around the sides of the bowl, then use tongs to dress the salad.

4. Transfer to a large serving platter. Drizzle with some of the remaining dressing, top with the goat cheese and the remaining 2 tablespoons pistachios and 1 tablespoon cranberries and serve immediately. Transfer any leftover dressing to an airtight container and store in the refrigerator for up to 7 days.

Roasted Beet, Corn, Feta, and Mint Salad

I love this salad in the summer. Roasting beets is the only way I know to coax out their naturally sweet flavors. When corn is in season on the East Coast—usually July, August, and September—my kitchen looks like a cornfield, just filled with ears of fresh corn in their green husks. I eat it almost daily. I grill it here, but you can also cook it indoors on a grill pan or just boil it in salted water for 2 to 3 minutes until tender. Mint is a cool addition here, but you could also use basil if mint isn't your thing.

1. Set an oven rack in the middle position and preheat the oven to 375°F.

2. Coat the beets lightly with 2 teaspoons of the olive oil, then wrap the red beets in one piece of foil and the gold beets in a separate piece of foil. Place on a baking sheet and roast until cooked through and tender, about 45 minutes.

3. Remove the beets from the oven, let cool for 10 minutes, then peel and slice into ½-inch-thick wedges. Transfer the roasted beets to two separate small bowls (red beets in one and gold beets in the other) and set aside.

4. Preheat a charcoal or gas grill to medium-high heat. Brush the corn with the neutral oil and season with salt and pepper. Grill, covered, until lightly charred on all sides and tender, 2 to 3 minutes per side. Let cool slightly, then cut the corn kernels from the cobs and place them in a medium bowl.

5. In another medium bowl, combine the mustard, vinegar, honey, and shallot and season with salt and pepper. Stream in the remaining ¼ cup olive oil slowly and whisk quickly to emulsify.

6. Add 1 tablespoon of the dressing to the red beets, 1 tablespoon of dressing to the gold beets, and 3 tablespoons of the dressing to the corn. Season each with salt and pepper and toss until combined. Fold half of the mint into the dressed corn.

7. Spoon the beets onto a large platter, then scatter the dressed corn over the beets. Drizzle with additional dressing, to taste, and top with the feta. Garnish with the remaining mint.

Serves 4

- 2 medium red beets, scrubbed
- 2 medium gold beets, scrubbed
- ¼ cup plus 2 teaspoons extra-virgin olive oil
- 3 large ears corn, husked
- 2 teaspoons neutral oil, such as avocado or canola
- Kosher salt and freshly ground black pepper
- 2 teaspoons Dijon mustard
- 3 tablespoons white wine vinegar
- 1 teaspoon honey
- 1 small shallot, minced
- ¼ cup lightly packed hand-torn fresh mint leaves
- 2 ounces feta cheese, lightly crumbled

Serves 4 to 6

½ small head **red cabbage,** shredded (about 3 cups)

½ small head **Savoy cabbage,** shredded (about 4 cups)

½ small head **napa cabbage,** shredded (about 4 cups)

2 medium **carrots,** grated on the large holes of a box grater (about 1 cup)

6 tablespoons **rice vinegar**

½ teaspoon **celery seeds**

1 teaspoon **sugar**

Kosher salt and freshly ground **black pepper**

¼ cup **vegetable oil**

3 tablespoons sliced **scallions**

3 tablespoons chopped fresh **flat-leaf parsley leaves**

Triple-Cabbage Slaw

This slaw sounds fancier than it really is. I just wound up with an array of cabbages in my fridge one day and decided it was time to go into slaw action. The crunchiness of the cabbages makes this a great way to upgrade any sandwich, burger, or lobster roll. Be sure to always have celery seeds on hand in your spice rack. I find them a must for any good slaw.

1. In a large bowl, combine the cabbages and carrots. In a small bowl, combine the vinegar, celery seeds, and sugar and season with salt and pepper. Stream in the vegetable oil slowly and whisk quickly to emulsify.

2. Pour the dressing over the vegetables and toss to coat. Season with salt and pepper. Let sit for 15 minutes at room temperature.

3. Use tongs to transfer the slaw to a large serving bowl. Fold in the scallions and parsley and serve.

Serves 4

2 teaspoons Dijon mustard

3 tablespoons red wine vinegar

1 teaspoon honey

1 teaspoon chopped fresh oregano leaves, plus whole leaves for garnish

1 small shallot, minced

Kosher salt and freshly ground black pepper

¼ cup extra-virgin olive oil

2 pounds assorted heirloom tomatoes, cut into slices ¼ inch thick

¼ cup grated ricotta salata cheese (about ½ ounce)

1 tablespoon chopped fresh flat-leaf parsley leaves

Heirloom Tomato, Oregano, and Ricotta Salata

This tomato salad is a great example of how a dish that takes just a handful of minutes to make can still be a total crowd-pleaser. It's all about the tomatoes. If they're at peak flavor, you win. In the summer, look for heirloom tomatoes at the market and buy an assortment of sizes and colors to add some visual interest. Ricotta salata isn't used enough in my opinion. I love its semi-firm texture and bright white color.

1. In a medium bowl, combine the mustard, vinegar, honey, oregano, and shallot and season with salt and pepper. Stream in the olive oil slowly and whisk quickly to emulsify.

2. Layer the tomato slices on a large platter and season with salt and pepper. Drizzle with the dressing and top with the ricotta salata. Garnish with the parsley and whole oregano leaves and serve.

Pita Chip Chopped Salad

Serves 4 to 6

Crushing store-bought pita chips (my go-to brand is Stacy's) in my hands and folding them into a ton of chopped vegetables and torn lettuces is one of my tricks when I'm making a big bowl of salad for a hungry crowd. My friends (and Sophie, too) usually ask for "pita chip salad" when given the option. It's the crunch they love most.

1. In a large bowl, combine the romaine, arugula, radicchio, chickpeas, cherry tomatoes, olives, cucumbers, dill, and most of the pita chips (reserve ⅓ cup for garnish). Season with salt and pepper, toss to combine, and set aside.

2. In a medium bowl, combine the mustard, vinegar, lemon zest, lemon juice, honey, and shallot and season with salt and pepper. Stream in the olive oil slowly and whisk quickly to emulsify.

3. Drizzle half of the dressing around the sides of the vegetable bowl, then use tongs to lightly dress the salad. Add additional dressing to taste. Fold in the ricotta salata and Parmigiano.

4. Transfer to a large serving bowl, drizzle with additional dressing to taste, and garnish with the reserved pita chips. Serve immediately.

1 romaine heart, finely chopped (about 4 cups)

2 ounces baby arugula, finely chopped (about 1½ cups)

½ small head radicchio, finely chopped (about 1½ cups)

¾ cup cooked chickpeas

1½ cups cherry tomatoes, quartered

¾ cup pitted mild green olives, such as Cerignola or Castelvetrano, coarsely chopped

2 Persian (mini) cucumbers, diced (about 1 heaping cup)

1 tablespoon chopped fresh dill

2 cups pita chips, lightly crushed

Kosher salt and freshly ground black pepper

2 teaspoons Dijon mustard

2 tablespoons white wine vinegar

Finely grated zest of 1 lemon

2 tablespoons fresh lemon juice

1½ teaspoons honey

1 small shallot, minced

⅓ cup extra-virgin olive oil

⅓ cup grated ricotta salata cheese

⅓ cup freshly grated Parmigiano-Reggiano cheese

Anatomy of a Chopped Salad

Sophie

So many of my childhood memories are of me sitting in the very last booth, next to the kitchen, at Mesa Grill. There was a dish on the menu called the "Sophie Chopped Salad," which I loved, but with a twist. The team would actually make me my own special version of the salad, which was all the good stuff—all the cheese, olives, and chickpeas—without the lettuce.

I loved growing up in restaurants, for so many reasons. But one very silly reason was because it was the only place I could get a snack! The thing about chefs is, they never stock snacks at home. My dad always had *ingredients*, but not snacks. After all, he could just make himself whatever he wanted. But when you're twelve and all you really want is some Goldfish or Oreos . . . it's an issue.

There were two exceptions to the snack rule at Dad's house. First, he always had potato chips—but those were specifically for burgers. (His Crunch Burger is so iconic, and now I can't eat a burger without potato chips on it.) Second, he always had pita chips. Those were probably for garnishing salads like this one. I've definitely evolved as a diner since those early days at Mesa—these days, I'm on board with lettuce—but my affection for salty snacks like pita chips remains the same.

Bobby

If you want your kids to eat salad, try throwing some salty chips on top. (This works for adults, too.) But a chopped salad is always a great option, chips or no chips. The greatest chopped salads are not just a bunch of vegetables and legumes thrown in a mixing bowl, though. A successful chopped salad requires good technique.

Make it uniform. Cut all your vegetables, greens, beans, cheeses, and crunchy things like croutons or cracked tortilla or pita chips to a uniform size. The satisfaction comes from getting a bite where all the elements are evenly balanced.

Don't be shy with the dressing. Chopped salads usually require a little more dressing than a classic salad.

Prep ahead. One thing I love about chopped salads is they can be made and even dressed a little further ahead of time than other, more delicate salads. This is great if you need to prep it in advance and store it in the fridge.

Vegetables

Grilled Sweet Potatoes
with Basil Vinaigrette

Serves 4

3 (10-ounce) sweet potatoes, peeled

Kosher salt

2 tablespoons fresh lime juice

6 tablespoons orange juice

½ cup tightly packed fresh basil leaves, chopped

½ cup tightly packed fresh cilantro leaves, chopped

2 teaspoons honey

Freshly ground black pepper

¼ cup plus 2 tablespoons neutral oil, such as avocado or canola

8 whole chiles de árbol (optional)

When it comes to potatoes, orange is the new brown, and grilled is the new roasted. I'll take a sweet potato over a regular old russet any day. In this preparation I used some fresh basil that was on its last legs and turned it into an herbaceous and bright dressing. Make sure you hit the potatoes with the dressing when they're still warm from the grill.

1. In a large pot, combine the sweet potatoes, cold water to cover by 2 inches, and 2 tablespoons kosher salt and bring to a boil over medium-high heat. Reduce to a simmer and cook until the potatoes are tender but still firm, 15 to 20 minutes. Use a slotted spoon to transfer to a plate lined with paper towels. Let cool slightly.

2. While the potatoes are cooling, in a blender, combine the lime juice, orange juice, basil, cilantro, honey, ½ teaspoon salt, and ⅛ teaspoon pepper. With the blender running, slowly add the ¼ cup of the neutral oil until emulsified. Season with salt and pepper and set aside.

3. Heat a small cast-iron pan over medium heat and toast the chiles de árbol (if using) until they are soft and pliable, about 3 minutes. Set aside.

4. Preheat a charcoal or gas grill to high heat.

5. Slice each potato into ½-inch-thick rounds. Brush the potato pieces with the remaining 2 tablespoons oil and season with salt. Grill until deeply charred in spots and just cooked through, 3 to 5 minutes per side. Transfer to a platter, drizzle with the vinaigrette, and sprinkle the toasted chiles de árbol (if using) over the top.

6. Store any leftover vinaigrette in an airtight container in the refrigerator for up to 5 days.

Roasted Sweet Potatoes with Date-Lime Butter

Roasted Sweet Potatoes with Chermoula-Honey Dressing

Roasted Sweet Potatoes with Sriracha-Scallion Butter

Roasted Sweet Potatoes, Three Ways

If you come over to my house, you'll notice a bowl of sweet potatoes is always on my counter. They're one of my favorite ingredients because they're good for you (at least that's what they tell me), vibrant, and versatile. Sometimes I go for the white-fleshed variety, sometimes orange, and then there's my new favorite, bright purple, which I discovered in Los Angeles. The potatoes have varying degrees of sweetness, which I like to complement with an additional sweet element and something tart or spicy to top them off. Here are three ideas, but play around with other sweet, tart, or spicy combos.

Roasted Sweet Potatoes
with Chermoula-Honey Dressing

Note: *Look for preserved lemons in stores specializing in Mediterranean or Middle Eastern ingredients, or in a well-stocked grocery store in the same aisle as the olives and capers.*

1. Set an oven rack in the middle position and preheat the oven to 450°F. Line a large baking sheet with parchment paper.

2. Drizzle the sweet potatoes with 3 tablespoons of the olive oil and season with salt and black pepper. Toss to combine. Roast until golden brown in spots and tender, 40 to 50 minutes, gently stirring the potatoes once, halfway through the cooking time.

3. Meanwhile, in a small skillet set over medium heat, toast the cumin and coriander seeds until fragrant, shaking the pan frequently, 4 to 6 minutes. Transfer to a small bowl to cool completely, then place in a spice grinder or mortar and grind to a fine powder.

4. In a food processor, combine the ground spices, garlic, mint, cilantro, parsley, preserved lemon, honey, lemon zest and juice, pepper flakes, and paprika. Pulse until coarsely chopped. With the food processor running, slowly stream in the remaining 6 tablespoons oil and blend until mostly smooth. Season with salt and black pepper.

5. Transfer the roasted potatoes to a platter and drizzle with some of the dressing. Garnish with additional mint, cilantro, and parsley. Serve immediately with any extra dressing served on the side.

Serves 4

- 4 (10-ounce) sweet potatoes, unpeeled, scrubbed, and cut into 1-inch pieces
- 9 tablespoons extra-virgin olive oil
- Kosher salt and freshly ground black pepper
- 1 teaspoon cumin seeds
- 1 teaspoon coriander seeds
- 2 garlic cloves, finely chopped to a paste with ¼ teaspoon kosher salt
- 2 tablespoons coarsely chopped fresh mint leaves, plus more for garnish
- ¾ cup coarsely chopped fresh cilantro leaves, plus more for garnish
- 1 cup coarsely chopped fresh flat-leaf parsley leaves, plus more for garnish
- 1 tablespoon finely chopped preserved lemon
- 1 tablespoon honey
- Finely grated zest and juice of 1 lemon
- ¼ teaspoon red pepper flakes
- ¾ teaspoon smoked paprika

Roasted Sweet Potatoes

with Sriracha-Scallion Butter

Serves 4

1. Set an oven rack in the middle position and preheat the oven to 425°F. Line a baking sheet with parchment paper.

2. Rub the sweet potatoes with the olive oil and season with salt and pepper. Place the potatoes on the lined baking sheet and roast until tender when pierced with a fork, 40 to 45 minutes, turning the potatoes over once, halfway through the cooking time.

3. Meanwhile, in a medium bowl, combine the butter, Sriracha, honey, and ¼ teaspoon salt. Stir to combine, then fold in half of the scallions.

4. Transfer the roasted sweet potatoes to a platter, split open with a knife, and slather with the butter. Sprinkle with more salt and the remaining scallions. Serve immediately with any extra Sriracha and scallion butter on the side. Store any leftover butter in an airtight container in the refrigerator for up to 5 days or in the freezer for up to 3 months.

4 (8-ounce) **sweet potatoes,** unpeeled and scrubbed

1 tablespoon **extra-virgin olive oil**

Kosher salt and freshly ground **black pepper**

1 stick (4 ounces) **unsalted butter,** at room temperature

1 tablespoon **Sriracha**

1 tablespoon **honey**

2 tablespoons sliced **scallions**

Roasted Sweet Potatoes

with Date-Lime Butter

Serves 4

1. Follow steps 1 and 2 above.

2. Meanwhile, in a medium bowl, combine the butter, half of the lime zest, the lime juice, date syrup, ½ teaspoon salt, and some pepper. Stir until smooth.

3. Transfer the roasted sweet potatoes to a platter, split open with a knife, and slather with the date butter. Sprinkle with more salt and pepper, then garnish with the toasted sesame seeds and the remaining lime zest. Serve immediately with any extra date butter on the side. Store any leftover butter in an airtight container in the refrigerator for up to 5 days or in the freezer for up to 3 months.

4 (8-ounce) **sweet potatoes,** unpeeled and scrubbed

1 tablespoon **extra-virgin olive oil**

Kosher salt and freshly ground **black pepper**

1 stick (4 ounces) **unsalted butter,** at room temperature

Finely grated zest of 1 **lime**

2 teaspoons fresh **lime juice**

2 tablespoons **date syrup** or **molasses**

1 teaspoon **toasted sesame seeds,** for garnish

Eggplant Parm

Eggplant is one of my favorite choices when meat isn't an option. So whenever there's a vegetarian in the house, this is my go-to Sunday night dinner. To make sure the eggplant remains the star of the show, don't overwhelm it with too much sauce and cheese. Roasting it before frying ensures that the interior of the eggplant is rich and custardy.

1. Set one oven rack in the upper third of the oven and a second oven rack in the bottom third and preheat the oven to 425°F. Line two baking sheets with parchment paper.

2. Arrange the eggplant slices in an even layer on the baking sheets. Brush both sides with the olive oil and season with salt and pepper. Place a baking sheet on each of the racks and roast until lightly golden brown and tender, about 20 minutes, turning the eggplant and switching racks halfway through the cooking time. Remove from the oven and let cool completely. Leave the oven on.

3. Meanwhile, pour the tomato sauce into a large saucepan and heat over medium heat until the sauce starts to simmer, about 5 minutes. Remove from the heat and cover with a lid to keep warm while you bread and fry the eggplant.

4. Fill a large cast-iron skillet halfway with neutral oil and heat over medium-high heat to 365°F on a deep-fry thermometer.

5. While the oil heats up, set up a dredging station and arrange the dishes in this order: In one shallow baking dish or large plate, place the flour and season with salt and pepper. In a second shallow dish, whisk the eggs and season with salt and pepper. In a third shallow baking dish, combine the plain bread crumbs and panko and season with salt and pepper.

6. Dredge a cooled eggplant slice first in the flour, shaking off the excess, then dip it in the eggs and dredge it in the bread crumb mixture. Shake off any excess breading and transfer the eggplant slice to a baking sheet. Repeat with the remaining eggplant slices.

7. Set up a wire rack in a sheet pan. Working in batches, fry the eggplant slices until golden brown and crispy, 1 to 2 minutes per side. Transfer to the wire rack and season with salt.

Serves 4 to 8

3 medium **eggplants** (about 3 pounds), cut lengthwise into 12 slices

¼ cup **extra-virgin olive oil,** plus more for the baking dish

Kosher salt and freshly ground **black pepper**

2½ cups **Basic Tomato Sauce** (page 243)

Neutral oil, such as avocado or canola, for deep-frying

1½ cups **all-purpose flour**

4 large **eggs,** beaten

1½ cups **plain dried bread crumbs**

1½ cups **panko bread crumbs**

2 cups shredded **low-moisture mozzarella cheese**

½ cup freshly grated **Parmigiano-Reggiano cheese,** plus more for garnish

¼ cup hand-torn fresh **basil leaves,** plus more for garnish

1 tablespoon chopped fresh **oregano leaves,** plus whole leaves for garnish

6 ounces fresh **mozzarella cheese,** thinly sliced

Recipe continues

8. Lightly brush the bottom and sides of a 13 × 9-inch baking dish with olive oil. Lay 4 of the largest slices of fried eggplant into the baking dish. Top each slice of eggplant with ¼ cup tomato sauce, ¼ cup shredded mozzarella, 1 tablespoon Parmigiano, ½ tablespoon basil, and sprinkle evenly with half of the oregano. Season with salt and pepper. Top with 4 more eggplant slices (lining them up with the bottom slices to create "stacks") and repeat the topping process. For the final layer, set the remaining 4 eggplant slices on top of the stacks, top each with 2 tablespoons tomato sauce, season with salt and pepper, and set slices of fresh mozzarella on top. You should have 4 eggplant stacks with 3 slices of eggplant each.

9. Set the baking dish on the top rack and bake until the cheese is completely melted and lightly browned in spots, about 15 minutes. Garnish with additional Parmigiano, hand-torn fresh basil, and whole oregano leaves. Serve immediately.

> **"**
>
> Whether it's his eggplant rigatoni from *Bobby at Home* (I don't have ALL his cookbooks, but I do have that one!) or this eggplant parm, my dad knows his way around an eggplant. It's one of those vegetables that I really don't know what to do with, but every time he prepares it, I think to myself, *I had no idea eggplant could taste so good!* —SF
>
> **"**

Curried Cauliflower
with Dukkah and Yogurt

Good-quality curry powder and a yogurt dipping sauce will up your cauliflower game immediately. Here I top it with dukkah, a Middle Eastern nut and spice mix. Botanica, a Los Angeles restaurant and market I really love, adds flakes of coconut to their dukkah. It's not necessarily traditional, but I love that subtle sweetness and have incorporated their twist here.

1. Set an oven rack in the lowest position and preheat the oven to 450°F. Line a baking sheet with parchment paper.

2. Make the cauliflower: In a large sauté pan, heat the neutral oil over medium-high heat. Add the shallot and cook until soft, 2 to 3 minutes. Add the garlic and ginger and cook for 1 minute longer. Turn off the heat and stir in the curry powder and brown sugar. Add the cauliflower, season with salt and pepper, and toss until evenly coated in the oil and spices. Spread out the cauliflower onto the prepared baking sheet.

3. Transfer the baking sheet of cauliflower to the oven and roast until golden brown and tender, about 30 minutes, turning the florets once, halfway through the cooking time.

4. Meanwhile, make the dukkah: Heat a medium sauté pan over medium heat. Spread the pumpkin seeds and hazelnuts in a single layer in the pan and toast, shaking the pan frequently, until lightly browned in spots, 6 to 8 minutes. Transfer to a bowl. Add the sesame seeds, cumin seeds, and coriander seeds to the pan and toast, shaking the pan frequently, until fragrant, 5 to 7 minutes. Add to the bowl with the nuts and seeds. Add the coconut to the pan and toast, stirring frequently, until light golden brown, 2 to 3 minutes. Transfer to a separate bowl. Allow the nut/seed mixture and the coconut to cool completely.

5. Once cooled, coarsely crush the nuts and seeds in a spice grinder or mortar. Transfer to the bowl with the toasted coconut and add ¼ teaspoon salt and ⅛ teaspoon pepper. Stir to combine.

6. To finish: Spread the yogurt onto the bottom of a large platter, season with salt and pepper, and top with the roasted cauliflower. Drizzle with olive oil and sprinkle some of the dukkah on top. Garnish with parsley leaves and quick-pickled red onions and serve.

Serves 4

Cauliflower

⅓ cup **neutral oil,** such as avocado or canola

1 small **shallot,** finely diced

2 **garlic cloves,** minced

1-inch piece fresh **ginger,** peeled and minced

1 tablespoon **curry powder**

1 teaspoon **light brown sugar**

1 large head **cauliflower** (about 2½ pounds), cut into florets

Kosher salt and freshly ground **black pepper**

Dukkah

3 tablespoons **pumpkin seeds**

¼ cup **hazelnuts,** skinned and roughly chopped

3 tablespoons **sesame seeds**

2 teaspoons **cumin seeds**

1½ tablespoons **coriander seeds**

2 tablespoons **unsweetened shredded coconut**

Kosher salt and freshly ground **black pepper**

To Finish

1 cup **2% plain Greek yogurt**

Kosher salt and freshly ground **black pepper**

Extra-virgin olive oil, for drizzling

Fresh **flat-leaf parsley leaves** and **Quick-Pickled Red Onions** (page 247), finely chopped, for garnish

Note: *Store any extra dukkah in an airtight container at room temperature for up to 2 weeks or in the freezer for up to 3 months.*

Turmeric Cauliflower Agrodolce
with Currants and Pine Nuts

For a lot of people, cauliflower isn't winning any vegetable popularity contests. But I'm not giving up the fight! All it needs is a little love, and my love language at the moment happens to be Italian. So here I bathe it in a sweet-and-sour sauce called agrodolce. What I like about this preparation is it allows the cauliflower to be cauliflower, in all its glory. You won't see me trying to turn it into rice or a pizza crust anytime soon.

1. Make the turmeric cauliflower: Set an oven rack in the lowest position and preheat the oven to 450°F. Line a baking sheet with parchment paper.

2. In a large sauté pan, heat the olive oil over medium heat. Add the garlic and cook until soft, about 1 minute. Remove from the heat and gradually stir in the brown sugar, turmeric, and paprika. Add the cauliflower, season with salt and pepper, and gently toss until evenly coated in the oil and spices. Spread out the cauliflower onto the prepared baking sheet.

3. Transfer the cauliflower to the oven and roast until golden brown and tender, about 30 minutes, turning the florets once, halfway through the cooking time.

4. Meanwhile, make the agrodolce: In a small saucepan, combine the vinegar, honey, and chiles. Bring to a boil over medium-high heat, then reduce to a simmer and cook until syrupy and reduced by more than half (about ½ cup), about 20 minutes. Season with salt, transfer to a bowl, and set aside.

5. To finish: Put the currants into a small bowl and cover with boiling water. Allow to sit and rehydrate until the currants are plump, about 5 minutes. Drain well.

6. Heat a small sauté pan over medium heat. Spread out the pine nuts in a single layer in the pan and toast until lightly browned in spots, shaking the pan frequently and tossing the nuts, 3 to 5 minutes. Transfer to a bowl and allow to cool slightly. Add the parsley and currants and stir to combine.

7. Drizzle the roasted cauliflower with half of the agrodolce and gently stir to coat. Transfer to a serving platter. Drizzle with additional agrodolce and sprinkle with the pine nut/currant mixture. Serve immediately.

Serves 4

Turmeric Cauliflower

⅓ cup **extra-virgin olive oil**

2 **garlic cloves,** finely chopped to a paste with ¼ teaspoon **kosher salt**

½ teaspoon **light brown sugar**

1 teaspoon **ground turmeric**

1½ teaspoons **smoked paprika**

1 large head **cauliflower** (about 2½ pounds), cut into florets

Kosher salt and freshly ground **black pepper**

Agrodolce

1¼ cups **red wine vinegar**

⅓ cup **honey**

2 **Fresno chiles,** thinly sliced

Kosher salt

To Finish

2 tablespoons **dried currants**

2 tablespoons **pine nuts**

2 tablespoons chopped fresh **flat-leaf parsley leaves**

Broccoli Rabe and Roasted Red Peppers

with Honey-Mustard Dressing

Serves 4

2 small **red bell peppers**

2 tablespoons **neutral oil,** such as avocado or canola

Kosher salt and freshly ground **black pepper**

1 heaping tablespoon **Dijon mustard**

3 tablespoons **white wine vinegar**

1 heaping tablespoon **honey**

1 small **shallot,** minced

⅓ cup **extra-virgin olive oil**

2 large bunches **broccoli rabe** (about 1½ pounds), woody stems trimmed

Okay, this is my favorite way to eat broccoli rabe. The key is the honey in the dressing, which counterbalances the pepperiness of the broccoli rabe. Roasted peppers give it that old-school Italian American vibe.

1. Preheat a charcoal or gas grill to high (or if cooking indoors, heat a grill pan or cast-iron skillet over high heat).

2. Brush the bell peppers with ½ tablespoon of the neutral oil, season with salt and pepper, and grill or sear, covered but turning occasionally, until charred on all sides and tender, about 10 minutes. Transfer to a bowl, cover tightly with plastic wrap, and let steam and soften for 15 minutes. Keep the grill, grill pan, or skillet at high heat.

3. While the peppers steam, in a medium bowl, combine the mustard, vinegar, honey, and shallot and season with salt and black pepper. Stream in the olive oil slowly and whisk quickly to emulsify.

4. Peel, seed, and thinly slice the peppers and place them in a bowl. Add 2 tablespoons of the dressing and season with salt and pepper. Toss to combine, then set the peppers and the remaining dressing aside.

5. Set up a large bowl of ice and water. Bring a large pot of salted water to a boil. Add the broccoli rabe and cook until crisp-tender, about 2 minutes. Immediately plunge into the ice water bath. Drain until almost dry but still slightly damp (a little bit of water helps the rabe steam).

6. Toss the broccoli rabe with the remaining 1½ tablespoons neutral oil and season with salt and pepper. Grill or sear the broccoli rabe until crisp-tender and slightly charred on both sides, about 1 minute per side.

7. Transfer the broccoli rabe to a platter, drizzle with some of the dressing, and add the roasted red bell peppers. Top with more of the dressing and serve immediately.

Cornmeal Fried Okra

Serves 4

1 cup **buttermilk,** well shaken

1¼ cups **cornmeal**

Kosher salt and freshly ground **black pepper**

8 ounces **okra,** halved lengthwise

Neutral oil, such as avocado or canola, for deep-frying

Ranch Dressing, (page 248), for serving

This might spark a debate, but the only way I want to eat okra (and a lot of it) is dredged in cornmeal and fried. I've recently joined the legions of fans obsessed with ranch dressing, and the fried okra is a great vehicle. This is a cool snack to serve at cocktail time.

1. Set up a dredging station. Put the buttermilk and the cornmeal into two separate shallow bowls. Season each with salt and pepper.

2. Set a wire rack in a sheet pan. Working in batches of 3 or 4, dip the okra into the buttermilk and allow any excess to drain off. Dredge in the cornmeal and shake off the excess. Put the okra pieces on the wire rack to sit while the oil heats up.

3. Set up a second wire rack in a sheet pan. Pour in enough oil to come halfway up the sides of a large cast-iron skillet. Heat the oil over medium-high heat to 375°F on a deep-fry thermometer.

4. In batches of 6 to 8, fry the okra until golden brown and crunchy, turning the pieces occasionally, 2 to 3 minutes. Remove the fried okra from the oil with a slotted spoon and transfer to the second wire rack to drain. Season with salt.

5. Serve hot alongside the ranch dressing.

— 66 —

One of the things I love about my dad's recipes is that he encourages readers to expand their palates and try new, unfamiliar vegetables. Okra might be a little intimidating if you've never had it before, but fried up and with ranch, it's impossible to resist. I admire the way Dad encourages people to look beyond the usual suspects like tomatoes and kale at the grocery store and to try something different. —SF

— 99 —

Smoky Collard Greens
with Chipotle

Serves 4

¼ cup apple cider vinegar

1 tablespoon honey

2 tablespoons finely chopped canned chipotle peppers in adobo sauce

1 small Spanish onion, peeled and halved

Kosher salt and freshly ground black pepper

2½ pounds collard greens, ribs discarded and leaves chopped

Collard greens are my favorite hearty green. I was taught many, many years ago to cook the greens for a long time in vinegar with a smoked ham hock. Trust me, it's a great method—but these days, with so many people eating strictly vegetarian, I started cooking mine with chipotle peppers instead. This way you still get some smoke flavor from the chiles, and the "pot liquor" has a bit of fire, too. If I'm serving any kind of low and slow barbecue, then collard greens and cast-iron cornbread will definitely join the parade.

1. In a large saucepan or soup pot, combine 2 cups water, the vinegar, honey, chipotle, and onion. Season with salt and pepper and bring to a boil over medium-high heat. Add the collard greens in large handfuls, letting each batch wilt slightly before adding more.

2. Reduce the heat to medium-low and cook, covered, until the collards are very tender, stirring occasionally, 1½ to 2 hours. Uncover and cook, stirring occasionally, until the liquid is reduced by half, about 8 minutes; discard the onion. Season with salt and pepper.

3. Transfer to a serving bowl and serve.

Cremini Mushroom and Escarole Soup

This is one of my favorite cold-weather soups because it's brothy, earthy from the mushrooms, and nourishing thanks to the escarole, which holds up really well in hot chicken stock. I love having weekend soup and sandwich days with Sophie. I'm usually watching a football game, and she's scrolling through Instagram.

1. In a large Dutch oven, heat the olive oil over medium-high heat until it starts to shimmer. Add the onion and cook until lightly browned in spots and soft, 5 to 7 minutes. Add the mushrooms and cook until tender and lightly browned, about 10 minutes. Add the garlic and pepper flakes and cook, stirring constantly, for 1 minute.

2. Add the escarole and season with salt and black pepper. Cook until just wilted, about 2 minutes. Add the chicken stock, parmesan rind (if using), beans, and oregano. Bring the soup to a boil over medium-high heat, then reduce to a simmer and cook until the escarole is tender, about 10 minutes. Stir in the sherry vinegar and season with salt and black pepper.

3. Ladle the soup into serving bowls. Top with lots of Parmigiano, garnish with parsley, drizzle with olive oil, and serve.

Serves 4 to 6

¼ cup **extra-virgin olive oil,** plus more for drizzling

1 large **Spanish onion,** chopped

12 ounces **cremini mushrooms,** thinly sliced (about 6 cups)

3 **garlic cloves,** chopped into a fine paste with ¼ teaspoon **kosher salt**

½ teaspoon **red pepper flakes**

1 head **escarole** (about 1 pound) or **kale,** leaves roughly chopped (about 10 cups, lightly packed)

Kosher salt and freshly ground **black pepper**

6 cups **chicken stock,** homemade (page 243) or store-bought

1 **parmesan rind** (optional)

2 (15-ounce) cans **cannellini beans,** drained and rinsed well

2 teaspoons chopped fresh **oregano leaves**

1 tablespoon **sherry vinegar**

Freshly grated **Parmigiano-Reggiano cheese,** for serving

Chopped fresh **flat-leaf parsley leaves,** for garnish

Falafel Bar
with Harissa Tahini and Pomegranate Yogurt

Sometimes I make falafel as an excuse just to make all the accompanying condiments: sweet and tart yogurt sauce, an "alternative" hummus made with white beans, pickled onions, and a spicy harissa tahini. When Sophie has her girl crew over, I make a falafel bar of sorts, which is a crowd-pleaser because it's fun and very healthy. Don't forget to warm up some pillowy pita to tuck everything into.

1. Make the falafel: Drain the chickpeas in a colander, then spread them out on a baking sheet lined with paper towels and let sit until they are completely dry, 10 to 20 minutes.

2. In a medium sauté pan, heat the olive oil over medium heat. Add the onion, season with salt and pepper, and cook, stirring constantly, until soft, about 8 minutes. Add the jalapeño and cook, stirring constantly, until soft, about 3 minutes. Add the garlic and cook until soft, about 30 seconds. Transfer to a small bowl and cool completely.

3. Put the chickpeas in a food processor and add the cooled onion mixture, lemon juice, cardamom, cumin, baking powder, 1¼ teaspoons salt, and some pepper. Process until the mixture is finely ground but not pureed, stopping to scrape the bowl as needed. Add the parsley and pulse several times until combined. Transfer the mixture to a bowl.

4. Form the mixture into about 16 balls the size of Ping-Pong balls (about 2 tablespoons each) and place on a large plate or baking sheet. Chill in the refrigerator while the oil heats up.

5. Fill a large cast-iron skillet halfway with neutral oil and heat over medium-high heat to 350°F on a deep-fry thermometer.

6. Set up a wire rack inside a sheet pan. Working in two batches, fry the falafel balls until deep golden brown and crispy, turning occasionally, 4 to 5 minutes. Using a slotted spoon, transfer the falafel to the wire rack and season immediately with salt.

Serves 4

Falafel

1 cup dried chickpeas, soaked in cold water in the refrigerator for at least 18 hours and up to 24 hours

1 tablespoon extra-virgin olive oil

½ small white onion, finely chopped

Kosher salt and freshly ground black pepper

1 jalapeño, finely chopped

3 garlic cloves, finely chopped to a paste with ¼ teaspoon kosher salt

1 tablespoon fresh lemon juice

¼ teaspoon ground cardamom

1½ teaspoons ground cumin

1½ teaspoons baking powder

3 tablespoons chopped fresh flat-leaf parsley leaves

Neutral oil, such as avocado or canola, for deep-frying

Harissa-Tahini Sauce

½ cup tahini, well stirred

2 to 3 tablespoons harissa, to taste

1 tablespoon fresh lemon juice, or more to taste

Kosher salt and freshly ground black pepper

Extra-virgin olive oil, for drizzling

Recipe and ingredients continue

7. Make the harissa-tahini sauce: In a food processor or blender, combine the tahini, harissa, lemon juice, and 2 tablespoons water. Season with salt and pepper. Blend until smooth, adding extra water, 1 tablespoon at a time, until the consistency is similar to thin yogurt. Transfer to a serving bowl and drizzle with olive oil.

8. Make the pomegranate yogurt: In a serving bowl, combine the yogurt, olive oil, 1 tablespoon water, and the mint and season with salt and pepper. Stir until smooth. Swirl in the pomegranate molasses. Drizzle with pomegranate molasses and garnish with chopped mint and pepper.

9. To serve: Heat a large cast-iron skillet over medium-high heat. Working with 1 pita at a time, toast the pitas until lightly charred in spots on both sides, about 2 minutes. Wrap the pitas in a kitchen towel to keep warm.

10. Serve the falafel balls with the tahini-harissa sauce, pomegranate yogurt, pitas, shredded lettuce, white bean hummus, and quick-pickled red onions.

Pomegranate Yogurt

1 cup 2% plain Greek yogurt

1 tablespoon extra-virgin olive oil

1 tablespoon chopped fresh mint leaves, plus more for garnish

Kosher salt and freshly ground black pepper

1 tablespoon pomegranate molasses, plus more for drizzling

For Serving

4 large whole-wheat pitas

Shredded lettuce, such as romaine or iceberg

White Bean Hummus (page 247)

Quick-Pickled Red Onions (page 247)

Panfried Asparagus, Two Ways

Spring is the season of green foods. That includes fava beans, fresh peas, and of course the king of spring vegetables, asparagus. Lately my favorite method for cooking asparagus is to start with a cold pan, rub asparagus with some olive oil and place it in the cold pan, then crank up the heat to high to blister the spears so they get a bit of char. You go from raw to cooked in 5 minutes. From there, you can go a couple of directions. Romesco is one of my favorite sauces, so whenever I make it, I save some extra for other vegetable dishes or grilled meats and chicken. Another option is to top the asparagus with crunchy bread crumbs and lemon, which work on almost anything. That's how I used it to "sell" the idea of eating asparagus to Sophie when she was a kid. It worked!

Panfried Asparagus
with Garlic-Lemon Bread Crumbs

Serves 4

1 pound **asparagus,** trimmed

1 tablespoon **extra-virgin olive oil**

Kosher salt and freshly ground **black pepper**

2 tablespoons **unsalted butter**

¼ cup **Toasted Garlic-Lemon Bread Crumbs** (page 248)

1. Rub the asparagus with the olive oil and season with salt and pepper. Place the asparagus in a single layer in a large sauté pan and set the pan over high heat. Cook until the asparagus is starting to blister on the first side, 3 to 4 minutes. Add the butter to the pan (it will get smoky), swirling the pan until the butter is melted. Continue to cook, turning the asparagus a couple of times, until the asparagus is blistered on all sides and the butter is speckled and browned, about 1 minute longer.

2. Use tongs to transfer the asparagus to a large plate, then drizzle the browned butter over the top. Sprinkle with the garlic-lemon bread crumbs and serve.

Panfried Asparagus with Garlic-Lemon Bread Crumbs

Panfried Asparagus with Romesco and Pecorino

Panfried Asparagus
with Romesco and Pecorino

Note: *To roast the bell pepper, follow steps 1 and 2 on page 198.*

1. Make the romesco: In a large sauté pan, heat 2 tablespoons of the olive oil over medium-high heat. Add the garlic and cook, stirring a few times, until lightly golden brown on both sides, about 3 minutes. Transfer to a food processor.

2. Add 2 tablespoons of the olive oil to the pan. Add the almonds and cook, stirring a few times, until lightly golden brown on both sides, about 3 minutes. Transfer to the food processor. Add the bread to the pan and cook, stirring a few times, until toasted and golden brown on all sides, about 3 minutes. Add the bread to the food processor. Add the remaining 1 tablespoon oil to the pan and add the roasted pepper and tomatoes and cook, stirring a few times, until the tomatoes are blistered in spots and soft, about 5 minutes. Transfer to the food processor.

3. Add the raisins, chiles, vinegar, and honey to the food processor and process until smooth. Taste and season with salt and pepper. Transfer the romesco to a bowl and set aside.

4. Make the asparagus: Wipe out the pan used to make the romesco. Rub the asparagus with the olive oil and season with salt and pepper. Add to the pan and set the pan over high heat. Cook until the asparagus is blistered in spots but still crisp-tender, 5 to 7 minutes.

5. Transfer the asparagus to a large plate, drizzle with oil, and top with some of the romesco sauce and the Pecorino Romano. Garnish with parsley leaves and serve. Transfer any leftover romesco sauce to an airtight container and store in the refrigerator for up to 5 days.

Serves 4

Romesco

5 tablespoons **extra-virgin olive oil**

6 **garlic cloves,** peeled

¼ cup **almonds**

1 slice **white bread,** crust removed, cut into small cubes

1 **red bell pepper,** roasted (see Note), peeled, seeded, and chopped into 1-inch pieces

2 **plum tomatoes,** seeded and chopped into 1-inch pieces

2 tablespoons **golden raisins,** soaked in boiling water until soft, drained

2 **dried New Mexico chiles,** soaked in boiling water until soft, drained, seeded, and coarsely chopped

3 tablespoons **red wine vinegar**

1 teaspoon **honey**

Kosher salt and freshly ground **black pepper**

Asparagus

1 pound **asparagus,** trimmed

1 tablespoon **extra-virgin olive oil,** plus more for drizzling

Kosher salt and freshly ground **black pepper**

2 tablespoons freshly grated **Pecorino Romano cheese**

Fresh **flat-leaf parsley leaves,** for garnish

Desserts
and Drinks

Strawberry Crostata

I'm a big fan of crostatas, an Italian style of open-faced tart. There are three reasons. One, they're beautiful. Two, they're delicious. And three, they're easy for a part-time pastry guy like me. Strawberry wrapped in flaky pastry always works.

1. Make the buttermilk pie dough: In a food processor, combine the flour, granulated sugar, salt, and butter. Pulse until the mixture resembles coarse meal. Add 2 tablespoons of the buttermilk and pulse until the dough starts coming together to form crumble-like pieces, adding additional buttermilk, 1 teaspoon at a time, if needed. Transfer the dough to a large piece of plastic wrap, then use your hands to pat into a 1-inch disk and wrap tightly. Refrigerate until the dough is completely firm, at least 1 hour and up to 2 days.

2. Make the strawberry filling: In a medium bowl, combine 2 tablespoons of the cane sugar and the lemon zest. Scrape in the seeds from the vanilla bean. Use your fingers to rub the mixture together to infuse the sugar with the vanilla and lemon. Add the strawberries and stir to coat. Set aside.

3. Set an oven rack in the lowest position and preheat the oven to 400°F. Line a large sheet pan with parchment paper. Remove the dough from the refrigerator and let it sit at room temperature to soften, about 10 minutes. Lightly dust a work surface with flour and roll out the dough into a 12-inch round about ⅛ inch thick. Transfer the dough to the lined pan.

4. Gently stir the lemon juice into the strawberries, then sprinkle with the remaining 2 to 3 tablespoons cane sugar and the cornstarch. Gently stir to coat until there are no remaining clumps of cornstarch. Use a slotted spoon to transfer the strawberries to the dough, leaving a 2-inch border all around. Fold the border in over the filling, pleating as you go and leaving the center of the crostata uncovered. Brush the edges of the dough with the buttermilk and sprinkle with the turbinado sugar.

5. Bake until the crust is deeply golden brown and the filling is bubbling and thickened, 45 to 55 minutes. Allow the crostata to cool on the baking sheet for 30 minutes.

6. While the crostata is cooling, make the vanilla bean whipped cream: In a large chilled bowl, combine the heavy cream and cane sugar. Scrape in the seeds from the vanilla bean. Whip until soft peaks form and dollop on sliced wedges of the crostata.

Serves 6

Buttermilk Pie Dough

1⅔ cups all-purpose flour, plus more for dusting

2 teaspoons granulated sugar

¼ teaspoon fine salt

1 stick (4 ounces) cold unsalted butter, cut into small cubes

¼ cup cold buttermilk, well shaken

Strawberry Filling

4 to 5 tablespoons pure cane sugar (depending on the sweetness of your berries)

Finely grated zest of 1 lemon

½ vanilla bean, split lengthwise

1 pound strawberries, hulled and halved or quartered (depending on size; about 3½ cups)

1 tablespoon fresh lemon juice

3 tablespoons cornstarch

1 tablespoon buttermilk

1 tablespoon turbinado sugar

Vanilla Bean Whipped Cream

1 cup cold heavy cream

1½ teaspoons pure cane sugar

½ vanilla bean, split lengthwise

Note: *If rhubarb is in season, it's never a bad idea to add some to the berry mix.*

Brioche Chocolate Bread Pudding

Serves 12 to 16

1 pound day-old brioche bread, cut into 1-inch cubes (about 13 cups)

3½ cups heavy cream

2 cups whole milk

¼ teaspoon fine salt

1¼ cups granulated sugar

2 teaspoons pure vanilla extract

12 ounces bittersweet chocolate, finely chopped

4 large eggs

2 large egg yolks

1 tablespoon unsalted butter, at room temperature

3 tablespoons turbinado sugar

Vanilla ice cream, for serving

Bread pudding: Those two words together might not sound like the most interesting dessert in the world, but once you add a rich custard and ganache made with good-quality chocolate, it's a whole new ball game. Sophie loves chocolate in general, so this is a great way to showcase one of her favorite ingredients while using up brioche that's in its last days. Before baking, make sure to let the assembled bread pudding sit for 1 hour at room temperature. This allows the custard to fully soak into the bread.

1. Set an oven rack in the middle position and preheat the oven to 325°F.

2. Spread out the cubed bread into a single layer on a large baking sheet. Bake in the oven until dried out and lightly browned in spots, 20 to 25 minutes. (Stir the bread two or three times during the baking time to ensure it browns evenly.) Remove the baking sheet from the oven and set aside to cool.

3. While the bread cools, in a medium saucepan, whisk together 2½ cups of the heavy cream, the milk, salt, granulated sugar, and vanilla extract. Bring to a simmer over medium-high heat, whisking frequently until the sugar has dissolved, about 10 minutes. Remove from the heat, add half of the bittersweet chocolate, and whisk until completely melted. Set the cream/sugar/chocolate mixture aside and allow to cool slightly.

4. Meanwhile, place the remaining bittersweet chocolate in a heatproof medium bowl. Pour the remaining 1 cup heavy cream into a small saucepan. Bring to a simmer over medium heat, then pour over the chocolate and let sit for 1 minute. Gently stir until smooth and set the ganache aside.

5. In a medium bowl, whisk together the whole eggs and egg yolks until smooth. Slowly add the reserved warm cream/sugar/chocolate mixture, whisking constantly. Strain the mixture through a fine-mesh sieve into a large bowl.

Recipe continues

6. Grease a 13 × 9-inch baking dish with the softened butter. Scatter half of the bread in a single layer in the baking dish. Pour half of the custard mixture over the bread and press down on the bread until it is submerged in the custard. Drizzle with 1 cup of the chocolate ganache (reserve the remaining ganache to use later as a topping). Top with the remaining bread and custard. Press down to submerge the bread. Some of the chocolate ganache will rise to the top and that is okay.

7. Allow the bread pudding to sit at room temperature for 1 hour, pressing down on the bread occasionally to make sure it is fully submerged in the custard.

8. Meanwhile, preheat the oven to 325°F.

9. Sprinkle the top of the bread pudding with the turbinado sugar. Make a bain-marie (water bath): Place the baking dish in a larger roasting pan and fill the outer roasting pan with hot tap water until it comes one-quarter of the way up the sides of the baking dish. Place the roasting pan in the oven and bake until the custard is set and a toothpick inserted into the center comes out clean, about 1 hour 20 minutes. Remove the baking dish from the oven and the water bath and cool on a wire rack for at least 30 minutes.

10. When ready to serve, gently rewarm the reserved chocolate ganache in a double-boiler or in a microwave on low. Drizzle over the bread pudding. Serve warm topped with vanilla ice cream.

Snickerdoodle Ice Cream Sandwiches

Makes 6 sandwiches

1½ sticks (6 ounces) unsalted butter

2 cups all-purpose flour

1 teaspoon baking soda

1½ teaspoons cream of tartar

¼ teaspoon fine salt

1 cup granulated sugar

⅓ cup packed light muscovado sugar

1 large egg

1 large egg yolk

2 teaspoons pure vanilla extract

1 tablespoon plus 1 teaspoon ground cinnamon

Pinch of cayenne pepper

2 pints premium vanilla ice cream, slightly softened

I've always loved this "cookie with the weird name." The first person to make them for me was Wayne Harley Brachman, the first pastry chef at my restaurant Mesa Grill in New York. I remember the whole kitchen smelled like spicy cinnamon. Turns out cinnamon's perfect running mates are a hint of cayenne and some nutty brown butter. The cookie is crispy just on the edges, chewy throughout. Get some vanilla ice cream or gelato, grab two cookies, and you know what to do.

1. In a small saucepan, melt the butter over medium heat. Cook, swirling occasionally, until speckled and golden brown, 6 to 10 minutes. Transfer the brown butter to a bowl and set aside to cool until it is no longer warm to the touch. It is ready to use once it is completely cool but still in its liquid form.

2. Meanwhile, in a medium bowl, combine the flour, baking soda, cream of tartar, and salt. Whisk to combine and set aside.

3. In a stand mixer with the paddle, combine the cooled browned butter, ¾ cup of the granulated sugar, and the muscovado sugar. Beat on medium-high speed until well combined, about 1 minute. Add the whole egg, egg yolk, and vanilla and beat again on medium-high speed until the mixture is smooth, lightened in color, and fluffy, about 3 minutes. Add half of the flour mixture and mix on low until just combined. Add the remaining flour mixture and mix again until just combined. Transfer the mixture to a medium bowl, cover with plastic wrap, and refrigerate for at least 4 hours and preferably overnight.

4. Remove the chilled dough from the refrigerator and let sit at room temperature until it softens enough so it can easily be scooped, about 15 minutes.

5. Meanwhile, set an oven rack in the middle position and preheat the oven to 400°F. Line two large sheet pans with parchment paper and set aside.

6. In a small bowl, whisk together the remaining ¼ cup granulated sugar, the cinnamon, and cayenne.

Recipe continues

7. Portion the dough into 12 equal balls—you can eyeball it or use a 1½-ounce ice-cream scoop. Roll each dough ball in the cinnamon/cayenne/sugar until well coated. When the dough balls have all been rolled once in the sugar mixture, repeat the process one more time. Transfer to the prepared pans, 6 per sheet, spacing them at least 2 inches apart. Do not flatten the cookies at all since they will spread out quite a bit as they bake.

8. Bake one baking sheet of cookies at a time until the cookies have puffed (the centers will still be soft) and the tops are cracked in spots, 10 to 13 minutes. Let the cookies cool on the baking sheet for 5 minutes, then transfer to a wire rack to cool completely.

9. Once the cookies are cooled, flip them over so they are flat side up. Place a large scoop of the vanilla ice cream on top of half of the cookies, then place a second cookie on top of the ice cream. Lightly press down on the ice cream to help the cookies adhere, then transfer all the ice cream sandwiches onto one of the parchment-lined pans the cookies were baked on and place in the freezer until the ice cream is completely frozen again, about 1 hour.

Pear-Cranberry Crisp

This is an easy autumn dessert that can certainly work for Thanksgiving or the holidays. Fresh cranberries are usually put into action only as a sauce to accompany turkey. I like using them throughout the season in cocktails as well as desserts.

1. Set an oven rack in the middle position and preheat the oven to 375°F. Brush a 3-quart baking dish with melted butter and set aside.

2. In a medium bowl, combine the flour and crystallized ginger. Use your fingers to coat the ginger in the flour. This will help to remove some of the stickiness from the crystallized ginger so it doesn't clump together. Add the oats, pecans, turbinado sugar, ⅓ cup of the muscovado sugar, ¼ teaspoon of the cinnamon, and the salt. Stir to combine, then drizzle with the melted butter. Use your fingers to stir and pinch the mixture into clumps and clusters. Refrigerate while you make the fruit filling.

3. In a large bowl, combine the cranberries and pears. Sprinkle with the cornstarch and gently toss to coat. Add the orange zest, orange juice, maple syrup, fresh ginger, allspice, and the remaining ¼ teaspoon cinnamon and ⅔ cup muscovado sugar and stir to combine. Scrape into the prepared baking dish, spread out the filling so it is even. Sprinkle with the chilled crumble topping.

4. Bake until the pears are tender, the filling is bubbling, and the topping is crispy and golden brown, 45 to 60 minutes (the bake time will depend heavily on how ripe your pears are).

5. Meanwhile, make the crème fraîche topping: In a small bowl, combine the crème fraîche, vanilla extract, and orange zest. Scrape in the seeds from the vanilla bean. Whisk to combine, then refrigerate for at least 30 minutes so that the flavors can meld.

6. Cool the baked crisp on a wire rack for 15 minutes, then serve warm topped with the crème fraîche topping and garnished with thinly sliced crystallized ginger.

Serves 8 to 10

1 stick (4 ounces) unsalted butter, melted and cooled slightly, plus more for the baking dish

¾ cup all-purpose flour

3 tablespoons finely chopped crystallized ginger, plus more thinly sliced for garnish

½ cup old-fashioned rolled oats

¾ cup coarsely chopped pecans

¼ cup turbinado sugar

1 cup light muscovado or light brown sugar

½ teaspoon ground cinnamon

¼ teaspoon fine salt

12 ounces fresh cranberries, thawed if frozen (about 3 cups)

2 pounds firm-ripe pears, such as Bosc, peeled and cut into slices ¼ inch thick (about 6 cups)

3 tablespoons cornstarch

Finely grated zest of 1 orange

⅓ cup freshly squeezed orange juice

¼ cup maple syrup

1 tablespoon finely grated fresh ginger

⅛ teaspoon ground allspice

Crème Fraîche Topping

1 cup crème fraîche

2 teaspoons pure vanilla extract

2 teaspoons finely grated orange zest

1 vanilla bean, split lengthwise

Pistachio Milkshakes

To make these shakes at home you'll need to first make your own pistachio butter, or do what I do and buy a good-quality jarred version. I get mine at a stand called Arnett Farms at the Hollywood Farmers' Market in Los Angeles. Be careful, though. You might end up hooked on pistachio butter!

Note: If using store-bought pistachio butter, you'll need 1 cup. Depending on the thickness of the brand you use, you might have to adjust the amount of milk and ice cream in the milkshake.

1. Make the whipped cream: In a large bowl, using an electric mixer, whip the heavy cream, sugar, and vanilla until soft peaks form. Set aside.

2. Make the pistachio butter: In a high-powered blender, combine the pistachios, olive oil, honey, and ½ cup water. Blend until the pistachios form a coarse paste. Leave in the blender.

3. Make the milkshakes: Add the milk to the blender and blend until smooth. Scoop the ice cream into the blender and blend again until smooth.

4. Pour into 3 or 4 serving glasses, top with the whipped cream, and sprinkle with chopped pistachios. Serve with a side of your favorite Italian cookies, if desired.

Serves 3 or 4

Whipped Cream

½ cup **heavy cream**

½ teaspoon **sugar**

¼ teaspoon **pure vanilla extract**

Pistachio Butter

2 cups **raw pistachios**

2 tablespoons **extra-virgin olive oil**

3 tablespoons **honey**

Milkshakes

⅔ cup **whole milk**

1 quart premium **vanilla ice cream**

Coarsely chopped **unsalted roasted pistachios,** for garnish

Italian cookies, for serving (optional)

Milkshake Memories

Bobby

Milkshakes will always be part of my diet because they are such a big part of my favorite childhood memories. My dad and I had a ritual when I was in the single digits where we would drink black-and-white milkshakes (that's vanilla ice cream with chocolate fudge syrup), pick up a burger or a hero, and head home to spend the day watching baseball on TV.

Of course I'm going to try to pass along my love for milkshakes to Sophie! She likes the B&W flavor, too, but now we've both expanded our milkshake palates to flavors like pistachio, espresso, cookies and cream, and deep rich chocolate. But I encourage people to riff and create their own signature milkshakes—they're always a crowd-pleaser.

Sophie

I don't think anyone eats more pistachio gelato than me and my dad. Combined, we probably hold the world record. The first time we traveled to Rome together when I was a kid, we were there for three days and visited *nine* gelaterias. I counted, because even then I remember thinking it was a bit ridiculous. My dad judges every gelateria in Italy by its pistachio flavor. Here in the US, his benchmark would probably be vanilla or chocolate. But in Italy, it's all about the pistachios.

He'll be the first to say that his favorite food is ice cream, but I'd argue that his favorite food is actually *milkshakes*. I enjoy a milkshake, but my dad LOVES a milkshake. He jokes about how we should open a combo milkshake and coffee bar in Los Angeles, to honor our two great loves (for him, milkshakes; for me, coffee). Maybe someday!

Pick a base flavor. Start with 1 to 1½ cups of ice cream per shake. You can keep it simple and go with chocolate or vanilla, or get a bit creative. I know Sophie will experiment with alternative milk ice creams, but I'm a traditionalist.

Pick a hero ingredient. It could be a fresh herb like mint, a compote made from seasonal fruit, spices like cinnamon or chile powder, or even a shot of booze like tequila or bourbon.

Thin it out. Add some milk to thin everything out (my preferred ratio is 95 percent ice cream, 5 percent milk), blend, and garnish as desired.

Make it look good! An extra bit of the hero ingredient or some crunchy nuts are never a bad idea.

Triple-Coconut Cream Pie

Coconut is another ingredient in the parade of my favorites—pistachio, pomegranate, mango, blackberries, and so on—that I lean on for eating happiness. So you won't be surprised to hear I incorporate coconut in three different places here: the crust, the filling, and the whipped cream topping. When Sophie was younger, she was not a fan of coconut at all. All that changed when she got older, and she can now be spotted with coconut gelato in one hand and coconut cream pie in the other. (Cue the Sophie eye roll.)

1. Make the coconut crust: In a large bowl, with an electric mixer, combine the butter and cane sugar and beat until light and fluffy, about 3 minutes. Add the egg yolk and blend until smooth and well combined.

2. Add the shredded coconut, flour, and salt and mix on low until combined and crumbly. Add the coconut milk and mix until the dough just comes together. The dough is ready when you can squeeze some of it in the palm of your hand and it holds together. Use your hands to form the mixture into a smooth dough and then transfer it to a 9-inch tart pan with a removable bottom.

3. Press the dough evenly into the bottom and up the sides of the tart pan, getting it as close to ⅛ inch thick as possible. Use the back of a drinking glass or a measuring cup to help get the crust nice and even. Trim any excess dough from the edges of the tart pan. Prick the crust all over with a fork and refrigerate for at least 2 hours and up to 8 hours.

4. Set an oven rack in the lowest position and preheat the oven to 350°F.

5. Put the tart pan on a baking sheet. Line the crust with parchment paper or aluminum foil and fill with rice or dried beans.

6. Bake until the edges of the dough start to feel dry and set, about 20 minutes. Carefully remove the parchment paper or foil and the rice or beans. Return to the oven and continue to bake until the edges of the crust are golden brown and the dough is cooked through, about 15 minutes longer.

Makes one 9-inch pie

Coconut Crust

1 stick (4 ounces) unsalted butter, at room temperature

¼ cup pure cane sugar

1 large egg yolk

3 tablespoons unsweetened shredded coconut

1½ cups all-purpose flour

½ teaspoon kosher salt

1 tablespoon canned full-fat coconut milk, well stirred

Coconut Pastry Cream

1½ cups canned full-fat coconut milk, well stirred

¼ cup sweetened cream of coconut, such as Coco López, well stirred

¼ cup pure cane sugar

3 tablespoons cornstarch

1 large egg

3 large egg yolks

1 teaspoon coconut rum

½ cup very cold heavy cream

Coconut Whipped Cream

¾ cups very cold heavy cream

2 tablespoons sweetened cream of coconut, such as Coco López, well stirred

1 tablespoon pure cane sugar

1 teaspoon coconut rum

¼ teaspoon pure vanilla extract

Unsweetened coconut flakes, toasted, for garnish

Recipe continues

7. Remove from the oven and cool completely on the baking sheet.

8. Make the coconut pastry cream: In a medium saucepan, combine the coconut milk and cream of coconut and bring to a simmer. Remove from the heat and set aside.

9. In a stand mixer with the whisk, combine the cane sugar and cornstarch and whisk until combined. Add the whole egg and egg yolks and whisk on high speed until the mixture reaches a pale yellow color and it drops down like ribbons when you lift the whisk, about 3 minutes.

10. With the mixer on the lowest speed, slowly pour in half of the hot coconut milk mixture. This will help "temper" the eggs. Then pour all the egg mixture into the coconut milk saucepan and return to medium heat. Whisk vigorously and constantly until the custard starts to bubble and thicken, about 5 minutes. Whisk in the coconut rum.

11. Place a bowl over a larger bowl filled with ice and water. Strain the pastry cream through a fine-mesh sieve into the bowl to remove any lumps. Place a layer of plastic wrap on the surface of the pastry cream to prevent a skin from forming. Refrigerate over the ice bath until cool and firm, 30 minutes to 1 hour.

12. While the pastry cream is chilling, clean the bowl and whisk of the stand mixer and place them in the refrigerator to chill. Add the heavy cream and whip on medium-high speed until it reaches stiff peaks, 1 to 2 minutes.

13. Whisk the chilled coconut custard until it is smooth. Gently fold in the whipped cream. Spoon the mixture into the pie crust and smooth out the top. Loosely wrap with plastic wrap and refrigerate for at least 4 hours and up to overnight.

14. Make the coconut whipped cream: In the stand mixer with the whisk, combine the heavy cream, cream of coconut, cane sugar, coconut rum, and vanilla and whip on medium-high speed until it reaches medium-stiff peaks, about 2 minutes.

15. Top the pie with the coconut whipped cream and garnish with toasted coconut flakes. Cut into wedges and serve.

— 66 —

This is my dad's dream dessert. Every year for his birthday, I try to get him a coconut cake because it's his absolute favorite. If I can't be there for some reason, I'll text whoever he's with: 'You got him something with coconut, right?!' —SF

— 99 —

Walnut Praline Tart

Serves 6 to 8

In the South, and especially in New Orleans, pralines are traditionally made with pecans. When I decided to make this tart for the first time, I didn't have any pecans—but I did find some walnuts lurking in the back of my pantry. Turns out toasted, earthy walnuts taste great with the gooey caramel of a classic praline. I served this to Sophie and her USC girls with her favorite cinnamon gelato.

1. Make the buttermilk pie dough: In a food processor, combine the flour, granulated sugar, salt, and butter. Pulse until the mixture resembles coarse meal. Add 2 tablespoons of the buttermilk and pulse until the dough starts coming together to form crumble-like pieces, adding additional buttermilk, 1 teaspoon at a time if needed. Transfer the dough to a large piece of plastic wrap, use your hands to bring the dough together, then pat into a rectangle 1 inch thick and wrap tightly. Refrigerate until the dough is completely firm, at least 1 hour and up to 2 days.

2. Remove the dough from the refrigerator and let it sit at room temperature to soften up a bit, about 10 minutes. Lightly dust a work surface with flour and roll out the dough into a 16 × 8-inch rectangle about ⅛ inch thick. Transfer the dough into a 13¾ × 4½ × 1-inch rectangular tart pan with a removable bottom. Evenly press the dough into the tart pan and trim any excess dough from the edges of the pan. If the dough cracks a little, that is okay. Just use a bit of the excess dough to fill in the cracks. Prick the crust all over with a fork and refrigerate for at least 1 hour and up to overnight.

3. Put a large baking sheet on an oven rack set in the lowest position and preheat the oven to 375°F.

4. Line the chilled crust with parchment paper or aluminum foil and fill with rice or dried beans. Put the tart pan onto the hot baking sheet and bake until the edges of the dough start to feel dry and set, 20 to 25 minutes. Carefully remove the parchment paper or foil and the rice or beans. Return to the oven and continue to bake until the edges of the crust are golden brown and the dough is cooked through, about 15 minutes longer.

Buttermilk Pie Dough

- 1⅔ cups all-purpose flour, plus more for dusting
- 2 teaspoons granulated sugar
- ¼ teaspoon fine salt
- 1 stick (4 ounces) cold unsalted butter, cut into small cubes
- ¼ cup cold buttermilk, well shaken

Walnut Praline Filling

- 1⅔ cups walnuts (about 5 ounces)
- 4 tablespoons cold unsalted butter, cut into small cubes
- ⅓ cup granulated sugar
- ⅔ cup packed light muscovado sugar
- ¼ teaspoon fine salt
- ½ cup cold heavy cream
- 1 tablespoon bourbon
- Pinch of freshly grated nutmeg

Cinnamon gelato, for serving

Recipe continues

5. Remove from the oven and cool completely on the baking sheet. Leave the oven on and reduce the oven temperature to 350°F.

6. Make the walnut praline filling: Spread the walnuts evenly on a baking sheet and toast in the oven until lightly browned and fragrant, 8 to 10 minutes, stirring occasionally. Remove, cool slightly, and coarsely chop. Set aside.

7. In a medium saucepan, combine 2 tablespoons of the butter, the granulated sugar, muscovado sugar, salt, and cream. Cook over medium-high heat, stirring frequently, until the butter has melted and the sugar has dissolved, about 3 minutes. Stop stirring and attach a candy thermometer to the side of the saucepan. Allow the mixture to come up to a boil, then cook until the temperature reaches 230°F, 5 to 8 minutes. Remove from the heat and whisk in the remaining 2 tablespoons butter, the bourbon, and nutmeg.

8. Cool for 5 minutes in the saucepan, then stir in the walnuts and pour the hot filling into the cooled crust. Spread out the filling so that it is even. Cool at room temperature until fully set, about 2 hours.

9. Unmold the tart, slice into pieces, and serve topped with cinnamon gelato.

Butterscotch Pudding

Serves 4

2½ cups whole milk

¾ cup heavy cream

4 tablespoons unsalted butter

⅔ cup packed light muscovado sugar

¼ teaspoon fine salt

3 tablespoons cornstarch

3 large egg yolks

1½ teaspoons pure vanilla extract

2 to 4 tablespoons good-quality Scotch (depending on your taste)

Coarsely chopped salted and roasted hazelnuts, for garnish

I grew up eating a lot of pudding, and I seem to have passed the pudding-craving gene down to Sophie. This one has a silky but dense texture and deeply toasted, rich caramel taste—that's what makes it butterscotch! That, and the actual Scotch. My feeling is, if you don't use at least a shot of real Scotch, it's not really butterscotch.

1. In a large saucepan, combine the milk and ½ cup of the heavy cream and bring to a simmer over medium heat, stirring occasionally, about 10 minutes. Remove from the heat and set aside.

2. In a large deep sauté pan, melt the butter over medium-high heat. Stir in the muscovado sugar and salt. Keep stirring until the sugar goes from grainy to melted, 2 to 4 minutes. Once the mixture is smooth, continue cooking, stirring constantly, until you see the first wisp of smoke, 30 seconds to 1 minute. Turn off the heat, then carefully stir in ½ cup of the hot milk mixture. Turn the heat to low and whisk until smooth, 1 to 2 minutes. Turn off the heat and gradually whisk the butterscotch mixture into the remaining milk and cream mixture in the saucepan until completely combined and smooth. Set the butterscotch aside.

3. Put the cornstarch in a medium bowl. Add the remaining ¼ cup heavy cream and whisk until smooth. Add the egg yolks and whisk again until well combined and smooth. Whisking constantly, slowly add 1 cup of the hot butterscotch to the egg yolks. This will help "temper" the egg yolks. Then pour all the tempered egg mixture into the saucepan with the remaining butterscotch.

4. Return to medium heat and whisk constantly until the custard starts to bubble and thicken, 8 to 12 minutes. Turn off the heat and whisk in the vanilla and Scotch.

5. Place a bowl over a larger bowl of ice and water and strain the pudding through a sieve into the bowl to remove any lumps. Place a layer of plastic wrap on the surface of the pudding to prevent a skin from forming. Refrigerate over the ice bath until cool and set, about 1 hour. (Alternatively, you can skip the ice bath and just chill the pudding in the refrigerator for several hours and up to overnight.)

6. Whisk the pudding until smooth and creamy and spoon into small serving cups or bowls. Sprinkle with the chopped hazelnuts and serve.

Pregame Rum Punch

Serves 8 to 10

4 cups blackberries (about 1 pound), plus more for garnish

¾ cup sugar

2 cups fresh blood orange juice

2 cups fresh pineapple juice

1 cup fresh pink grapefruit juice

½ cup fresh lime juice

1 (750 ml) bottle Jamaican white rum

Ice cubes or ice ring (see Note)

Fresh mint leaves, for garnish

Orange, blood orange, and/or lime slices, for garnish

Sophie really taught me how to "pregame" on game-day Saturdays when she was going to college at USC in Los Angeles. Apparently, there's an art to it. You need to organize your cocktails, you need the right outfit, and you need to make a lot of whatever you're drinking because everyone at the party will want to check out your concoction. Clearly, both Sophie and my days of pregaming at college are over, but this punch will be a winner at any warm-weather outing. Even something a little less raucous, like a picnic!

Note: To make an extra-large ice ring for a punch bowl, fill a Bundt pan (make sure it is slightly smaller than the diameter of your punch bowl) with water and add sliced fruit, berries, and mint sprigs. Freeze overnight, then quickly run the bottom of the pan under some warm water, invert the ice, and add to your punch bowl right before serving.

1. In a medium saucepan, combine the blackberries, sugar, and ½ cup water. Bring to a boil over medium-high heat, stirring occasionally. Reduce the heat to a simmer and cook for 5 minutes, using a potato masher to lightly crush the berries as they cook. Pour the mixture through a fine-mesh sieve set over a bowl. Use the back of a spoon to help push down on the solids. Transfer the blackberry syrup to the refrigerator and cool completely.

2. In a large pitcher or punch bowl, combine the cooled blackberry syrup, blood orange juice, pineapple juice, pink grapefruit juice, lime juice, and white rum. Stir it all together, then refrigerate for at least 1 hour before serving.

3. Add the ice to the pitcher or punch bowl and garnish with the mint leaves and additional blackberries and citrus slices. Serve immediately.

This is probably a little more elevated than what *I* would typically serve at a pregame party. But I do love blackberries in my cocktails. If I ever see a drink on a menu with blackberries in it, I'm ordering it. —SF

Amalfi Spritz

Makes 1 cocktail

The signature drink of my restaurant Amalfi is this aptly named spritz. A spritz is a style of drink made with sparkling wine and some bittersweet liqueur, for example Aperol or Campari. It's made a tremendous comeback over the last few years. No matter how you're concocting your spritz, make sure you use a sparkling wine (Italian, if you want to stick with the theme) that you love. It's the foundation and it needs to taste great! Sophie and her girlfriends love hanging in the lounge of the restaurant and trying every spritz we have. They think of it as a spritz tasting menu.

Ice cubes

1½ ounces **Aperitivo Cappelletti**

3 ounces **dry sparkling white wine**

1 to 2 ounces **club soda**

Orange half-moon, for garnish

Fill a spritz glass or large red wineglass with ice cubes. Add the Cappelletti, then top with the sparkling wine and club soda. Use a long bar spoon to stir everything together, making sure to reach the bottom of the glass in order to pull up the Cappelletti. Nestle the orange half-moon between the ice and the drinking glass, then gently push it down into the drink. Serve immediately.

Mezcal Mule

Makes 1 cocktail

This cocktail has Sophie Flay written all over it. As soon as she was legal to drink, Sophie's go-to call over the bar was a Moscow Mule, a classic made with vodka, ginger beer, and lime. A couple of years ago she discovered her affection for the smoky, rich Mexican spirit mezcal, which inspired us to create this Mule remix. It really works.

1 ounce **mezcal**

1½ ounces **silver tequila** (my favorite is El Jimador blanco)

½ ounce fresh **lime juice**

Ice

4 ounces **ginger beer**

1 **lime wheel**

In a copper mug or glass, combine the mezcal, tequila, and lime juice and stir together. Add ice to fill the mug or glass. Top with the ginger beer, garnish with the lime wheel, and serve immediately.

Limonata

Makes 1 cocktail

No Italian vacation is complete without some lemony refreshment. So when I opened Amalfi, my coastal Italian restaurant in Las Vegas, I knew I wanted to feature a cocktail that reminded me of a perfect summer day on the Tyrrhenian Sea. Think of this as an Italian version of a mojito. Because lemons are such a huge part of the agriculture of the Amalfi Coast, we substituted lemons for the limes and added a couple of other twists to make it our own. It's so refreshing . . . and so easy to drink, so be careful!

3 **lemon wedges**

4 fresh **mint leaves**

Dash of **Simple Syrup** (recipe follows)

1½ ounces **white rum**

Ice cubes

2 to 3 ounces **sparkling Italian lemon soda,** such as San Pellegrino Limonata

In a chilled collins glass, combine the lemon wedges and mint leaves. Use a muddler or the handle of a wooden spoon to muddle the lemon and mint together. Add the simple syrup and white rum, then fill the glass with ice cubes. Top off with the sparkling Italian lemon soda. Use a long bar spoon to give everything a quick stir and serve immediately.

Simple Syrup

Makes 1½ cups

1 cup **sugar**

In a small saucepan, combine the sugar and 1 cup water. Bring to a boil over high heat and cook until the sugar has completely dissolved, about 3 minutes. Transfer the syrup to a container with a lid and refrigerate until cold. It can be stored in the refrigerator for up to 1 month.

Mezcal Mule

Limonata

Amalfi Spritz

Basics

Chicken Stock

Shrimp Stock

Basic Tomato Sauce

Chicken Stock

Makes about 6 cups

Whenever you roast a chicken (or buy a rotisserie chicken from the store), save the carcass in a plastic zip-top bag in the freezer. Your future self will thank you once you have enough to make a beautiful homemade stock.

5 pounds **chicken carcasses,** rinsed well

1 pound **chicken wings,** rinsed well

1 large **Spanish onion,** unpeeled, cut into 1-inch chunks

2 large **carrots,** cut into 1-inch pieces

2 **celery stalks,** cut into 1-inch pieces

8 sprigs **flat-leaf parsley leaves**

2 teaspoons **kosher salt**

1 teaspoon **black peppercorns**

1. In a stockpot, combine the chicken carcasses, chicken wings, onion, carrots, celery, parsley, salt, peppercorns, and 4 quarts cold water. Bring to a boil, then reduce the heat to low and simmer gently, skimming the surface occasionally, until the stock has reduced by one-third, 2½ to 3 hours.

2. Strain the stock through a fine-mesh sieve set over a large bowl or a clean pot (discard the solids). Use immediately, or let cool completely, transfer to airtight containers, and store in the refrigerator for up to 3 days or in the freezer for up to 3 months.

Shrimp Stock

Makes 6 cups

When I make a dish with shrimp, I always make sure to buy shell-on shrimp, which I peel myself so I have shells for stock. Even if I don't feel like making stock right away, I can freeze the shells for later and make the stock when I've accumulated enough.

Shrimp shells from 3 pounds shrimp

1½ large **Spanish onions,** diced

15 **black peppercorns**

3 **bay leaves**

1½ teaspoons **tomato paste**

1. In a large saucepan, combine the shrimp shells, onions, peppercorns, bay leaves, and 6 cups water. Stir in the tomato paste until

well incorporated, then bring to a boil over medium-high heat. Reduce to a low simmer, cover, and cook for 30 minutes. As the stock cooks, crush the shrimp shells with a potato masher or the back of a wooden spoon for maximum flavor extraction.

2. Pour the stock through a fine-mesh sieve set over a large bowl, pressing down on the shells even further, until all the liquid has been extracted (discard the solids). Use immediately, or let cool completely, transfer to airtight containers, and store in the refrigerator for up to 3 days or in the freezer for up to 3 months.

Basic Tomato Sauce

Makes 5 to 6 cups

Everyone should have a good, workhorse tomato sauce. This one is pretty classic, which is why it works for so many things: spaghetti and meatballs, eggplant parm, et cetera. I like a little heat in mine, but you can omit the red pepper flakes for a milder sauce.

3 tablespoons **extra-virgin olive oil**

1 large **Spanish onion,** finely diced

3 **garlic cloves,** coarsely chopped

½ teaspoon **red pepper flakes** (optional)

2 (28-ounce) cans whole peeled **plum tomatoes with their juices**

Pinch of **sugar**

2 tablespoons chopped fresh **flat-leaf parsley leaves**

2 tablespoons chopped fresh **basil leaves**

1. In a large saucepan, heat the olive oil over medium-high heat. Add the onion and cook until soft, 3 to 4 minutes. Add the garlic and pepper flakes (if using) and cook until soft, about 1 minute. Add the tomatoes and their juices and bring to a boil. Reduce to a simmer and add the sugar. Cook until the sauce is reduced and thickened, 45 minutes to 1 hour, using a potato masher to lightly crush the tomatoes as they cook.

2. Stir in the parsley and basil. Use immediately, or let cool completely, transfer to airtight containers, and store in the refrigerator for up to 3 days or in the freezer for up to 1 month.

Arugula Pesto

Makes about 1 cup

When it comes to pesto, why stop at basil? Other greens work great, too—especially arugula, with its spicy kick.

1 **garlic clove,** peeled

2 cups packed **baby arugula** (about 2 ounces)

1 cup packed fresh **flat-leaf parsley leaves**

3 tablespoons **pine nuts**

½ cup freshly grated **Parmigiano-Reggiano cheese**

Kosher salt and freshly ground **black pepper**

½ cup **extra-virgin olive oil**

1. In a food processor, pulse the garlic a few times to chop. Add the arugula, parsley, pine nuts, and Parmigiano and season with salt and pepper. Pulse several times until coarsely chopped. With the food processor running, slowly stream in the olive oil and blend until smooth. Taste and add more salt and pepper if needed.

2. Use immediately, or transfer to an airtight container and store in the refrigerator for up to 3 days or in the freezer for up to 1 month.

Shishito Pesto

Makes about 1½ cups

I have yet to meet a green or herb that I haven't tried to turn into a pesto. But lately I've been taking it a step further and adding peppers to the mix, too. If you want pesto with a bite, shishito peppers are a great option.

8 ounces **shishito peppers**

3 **garlic cloves,** peeled

1 cup packed fresh **basil leaves**

¼ cup **pine nuts**

⅓ cup freshly grated **Parmigiano-Reggiano cheese**

Kosher salt and freshly ground **black pepper**

⅓ cup **extra-virgin olive oil**

1. Place the shishito peppers in a single layer in a large deep sauté pan. Add ½ cup water and turn the heat to medium-low. When the water just starts to steam, cover with a lid and gently cook until the peppers are tender, 10 to 15 minutes. Transfer the peppers to a cutting board and cool completely.

2. Once cooled, cut away and discard the stems. Put the garlic in a food processor and pulse a few times to chop. Add the cooled shishitos, basil, pine nuts, and Parmigiano and season with salt and pepper. Pulse several times until coarsely chopped. With the food processor running, slowly stream in the olive oil and blend until smooth. Season with additional salt and pepper if needed.

3. Use immediately or transfer to airtight container, and store in the refrigerator for up to 3 days or in the freezer for up to 1 month.

Tomato–Red Chile Sauce

Makes about 3 cups

I'll often have two tomato sauces in my fridge or freezer, the basic Italian-style one on page 243 and this spicy version. Pasilla chile powder can be purchased at many Mexican grocery stores and online. If you can't find it, sub another high-quality red chile powder.

2 tablespoons **neutral oil,** such as avocado or canola

1 small **Spanish onion,** finely diced

4 **garlic cloves,** finely chopped

1 (28-ounce) can whole peeled **plum tomatoes with their juices**

1 tablespoon **ground cumin**

2 tablespoons **ancho chile powder**

2 tablespoons **pasilla chile powder**

2 tablespoons pureed canned **chipotle peppers in adobo sauce**

2 tablespoons **honey**

1 tablespoon fresh **lime juice**

Kosher salt and freshly ground **black pepper**

1. In a medium saucepan, heat the neutral oil over medium-high heat. Add the onion and cook until soft, about 5 minutes. Add the garlic and cook until soft, about 1 minute.

2. Add the tomatoes, cumin, ancho chile powder, pasilla chile powder, pureed chipotle, and honey. Use a potato masher to lightly crush the tomatoes against the sides of the pan. Simmer, stirring occasionally, until the sauce is thickened, 20 to 25 minutes.

Recipe continues

Shishito Pesto

Tomato–Red Chile Sauce

Arugula Pesto

**Quick–Pickled
Red Onions**

Guacamole

3. Transfer the mixture to a blender, remove the steam vent from the center of the lid and cover the small opening with a kitchen towel (this will help to release steam). Blend until smooth. Add the lime juice and season with salt and pepper.

4. Use immediately, or let cool completely, transfer to airtight container, and store in the refrigerator for up to 5 days or in the freezer for up to 3 months.

Quick-Pickled Red Onions

Makes about 1½ cups

This is one of my most-used condiments. Keep these in your fridge and you are always ready for taco night.

½ cup fresh lime juice

½ cup distilled white vinegar

1 tablespoon sugar

2 teaspoons kosher salt

1 red onion, peeled, halved, cut into ⅛-inch-thick half-moons

1. In a small saucepan, stir together the lime juice, vinegar, sugar, and salt. Bring to a boil over medium-high heat. Once the sugar and salt have dissolved, remove from the heat and let the mixture cool slightly.

2. Place the onions in a large heatproof bowl and carefully pour the liquid over the onions. Cover and refrigerate for at least 30 minutes.

3. Transfer to an airtight container and store in the refrigerator for up to 3 months.

Guacamole

Makes about 2 cups

Homemade guacamole is so easy and so good, it makes you wonder why you ever even looked at the prepared version they sell at the store.

2 Hass avocados, diced

3 tablespoons finely chopped fresh cilantro leaves

3 tablespoons finely diced red onion

1 jalapeño, seeded (optional) and finely diced

Juice of 1 lime

Kosher salt and freshly ground black pepper

In a medium bowl, combine the avocados, cilantro, red onion, jalapeño, and lime juice and season with salt and pepper. Use a fork to coarsely mash the avocado. Serve immediately.

White Bean Hummus

Makes about 1½ cups

Chickpeas are the traditional choice for hummus, but sometimes you just have to work with what you have. When I made this, all I had on hand were white cannellini beans. They make a creamy and slightly mellower hummus.

1 (15-ounce) can cannellini beans, drained and rinsed well

1 garlic clove, finely chopped to a paste with ⅛ teaspoon kosher salt

2 tablespoons fresh lemon juice

¼ cup tahini, well stirred

¼ cup extra-virgin olive oil, plus more for garnish

2 tablespoons chopped fresh flat-leaf parsley leaves, plus more for garnish

Pinch of chile de árbol powder or cayenne pepper

Kosher salt and freshly ground black pepper

1. In a food processor, combine the beans and garlic. Pulse until coarsely chopped. Add the lemon juice, tahini, and olive oil and pulse until almost smooth. Add the parsley and chile de árbol powder and season with salt and pepper. Pulse several times until just incorporated. If the mixture is very thick, add water, 1 tablespoon at a time, and pulse until the desired consistency. Season with additional salt and pepper if needed. Garnish with olive oil and parsley to serve.

2. Transfer to an airtight container and store in the refrigerator for up to 5 days.

Toasted Garlic-Lemon Bread Crumbs

Makes about ½ cup

I call for panko here, but this is also a great way to use up stale bread: Just tear it into pieces and blitz it in a food processor.

1 tablespoon extra-virgin olive oil

1 tablespoon unsalted butter

1 garlic clove, finely chopped to a paste with a pinch of kosher salt

½ cup panko bread crumbs

Kosher salt and freshly ground black pepper

Finely grated zest of 1 lemon

1. In a large sauté pan, heat the olive oil and butter over medium heat until the butter has melted and the mixture begins to shimmer. Add the garlic and cook, stirring constantly, until soft, about 1 minute.

2. Add the panko, season with salt and pepper, and cook, stirring occasionally, until golden brown and toasted, 6 to 10 minutes. Stir in the lemon zest and transfer to a plate in an even layer to cool.

3. Store the bread crumbs in an airtight container in a cool, dark place for up to 2 days. To re-crisp, spread bread crumbs on a baking sheet and toast in a 300°F oven for 5 minutes.

Pantry Barbecue Sauce

Makes about 1½ cups

Here's a very straightforward sauce you can pull together with ingredients you probably already have on hand in your pantry and fridge, for all your emergency barbecue needs. Use whatever mustard, sugar, hot sauce, and vinegar you have on hand—it's all good.

1 cup ketchup

3 tablespoons honey

2 tablespoons mustard

2 tablespoons brown sugar

1 tablespoon hot sauce

1 tablespoon soy sauce

1 tablespoon vinegar

1 tablespoon Worcestershire sauce

½ teaspoon cayenne pepper

Kosher salt

1. In a medium saucepan, combine the ketchup, honey, mustard, brown sugar, hot sauce, soy sauce, vinegar, Worcestershire sauce, and cayenne and bring to a boil over medium-high heat. Reduce to a simmer, cover, and cook for 20 minutes, stirring occasionally.

2. Season to taste with salt and taste for balance. If the sauce needs more sweetness, add more honey. If it needs more heat, add more hot sauce. If it gets too thick, add a splash of water.

3. Store, tightly covered, in the refrigerator for up to 5 days or in the freezer for up to 6 months.

Ranch Dressing

Makes about 1 cup

For a long time, I didn't really get the obsession with ranch dressing. That was until I started making my own at home. Now I get it and I'm fully on board.

½ cup buttermilk, well shaken

3 tablespoons mayonnaise

3 tablespoons sour cream

1 tablespoon fresh lime juice

2 garlic cloves, finely chopped to a paste with ¼ teaspoon kosher salt

2 tablespoons thinly sliced fresh chives

2 tablespoons finely chopped fresh cilantro leaves

2 teaspoons finely chopped fresh dill

1 teaspoon kosher salt

⅛ teaspoon cayenne pepper

In a medium bowl, combine all the ingredients and whisk to combine. Serve immediately, or transfer to an airtight container and store in the refrigerator for up to 5 days.

> I feel like my dad is new to ranch; he is only *just* accepting that it is the best thing on the planet. So I love that he has his own homemade version now. —SF

**Pantry
Barbecue Sauce**

**Ranch
Dressing**

**Toasted
Garlic–Lemon
Bread Crumbs**

**White Bean
Hummus**

Acknowledgments

Below is a list of people who deserve special recognition for their hard work and dedication to this project. I'm a lucky person to be associated with such a talented circle of professionals who help bring my culinary passions to life. I appreciate each and every one of you.

Sophie Flay
Emily Timberlake
Sally Jackson
Christine Sanchez
Ed Anderson
Elyse King
Christie Bok
Dagne Aiken
Renee Forsberg
Susan Vu
Dahlia Warner
Courtney Fuglein
Maeve Sheridan
Julia Memoli
Valerie Aikman-
  Smith
Tuyen Tran
Jun Tan
Karen Perez
Rebecca Strzelinski
Chrystal Baker
Munah Gomes

LJ Almendras
Laurence Kretchmer
Irika Slavin
Jennifer Sit
Ian Dingman
Marysarah Quinn
Kate Tyler
Haley Jackson
Bianca Cruz
Lydia O'Brien
Susan Roxborough
Food Network
Stephanie Davis
Joyce Wong
Yosmar Brito
Kalamazoo Grills
Laura Sommers
KitchenAid
Mandy Ruholl-Cook
Boos Board
Adèle Schober
Breville

Index

Note: Page references in *italics* indicate photographs.

Grateful acknowledgment is made to the following for permission to reprint previously published material:
Samin Nosrat: Recipe adaptation of "Scrambled Eggs with Prosciutto and Focaccia" by Samin Nosrat, originally appeared on saltfatacidheat .com. Copyright © Samin Nosrat. Reprinted by permission of Samin Nosrat.
Clarkson Potter/Publishers: Recipe adaptation of "Skillet-roasted Lemon Chicken" from *Cooking for Jeffrey: A Barefoot Contessa Cookbook* by Ina Garten, copyright © 2016 by Ina Garten. Reprinted by permission of Clarkson Potter/Publishers, an imprint of Random House, a division of Penguin Random House LLC. All rights reserved.

Library of Congress Cataloging-in-Publication Data has been applied for.

ISBN 978-0-593-23240-8
Ebook ISBN 978-0-593-23241-5

Printed in China

Photographer: Ed Anderson
Editor: Jennifer Sit
Assistant Editor: Lydia O'Brien
Editorial Assistant: Bianca Cruz
Designer: Ian Dingman
Production Editor: Joyce Wong
Production Manager: Kelli Tokos
Compositors: Merri Ann Morrell, Nick Patton, and Hannah Hunt
Copy Editor: Kate Slate
Indexer: Elizabeth Parson
Marketer: Stephanie Davis
Publicist: Kate Tyler and Jana Branson

10 9 8 7 6 5 4 3 2 1

First Edition